The Psychology of Success

KEYS TO A SUCCESSFUL AND HAPPIER LIFE

G. A. MOHR,

P.E. MOHR & R.S. MOHR

The Psychology of Success

KEYS TO A SUCCESSFUL AND HAPPIER LIFE

G. A. MOHR,

P.E. MOHR & R.S. MOHR

G. A. Mohr, P.E Mohr & R.S. Mohr
The Psychology of Success
Keys to a successful and happier life.

TRI

Transworld Research & Innovation
9 Hampstead Drive
Hoppers Crossing VIC 3029
AUSTRALIA

ALSO BY G. A. MOHR

Finite Elements for Solids, Fluids, and Optimization

A Microcomputer Introduction to the Finite Element Method

The Pretentious Persuaders,
A Brief History & Science of Mass Persuasion

Curing Cancer & Heart Disease,
Proven Ways to Combat Aging, Atherosclerosis & Cancer

The Variant Virus, Introducing Secret Agent Simon Sinclair

The Doomsday Calculation, The End Of The Human Race

The War of the Sexes, Women Are Getting On Top

Heart Disease, Cancer, & Ageing:
Proven Neutraceutical & Lifestyle Solutions

2045: A Remote Town Survives Global Holocaust

The History & Psychology of Human Conflict

Elementary Thinking for Modern Management

The 8-Week+ Program to Reverse Cardiovascular Disease

The Scientific MBA;   Mohr's Law of Hierarchies

The DIY Cardiovascular Cure,
A Comprehensive Program to Reverse Atherosclerosis

Combating Cancer, Proven Neutraceutical & Lifestyle Remedies

ALSO WITH R.S. MOHR/RICHARD SINCLAIR & P.E. MOHR/EDWIN FEAR

The Evolving Universe: Relativity, Redshift and Life from Space

World Religions: The History, Psychology, Issues & Truth

World War 3, When & How Will It End?

The Brainwashed, From Consumer Zombies to Islamic Jihad

Human Intelligence, Learning & Behaviour

The Psychology of Hope

New Theories of The Universe, Evolution, and Relativity

The Population Explosion

World Religions: From to Animism to Mohronism

Human Conflict: An Attitudinal Psychology Model

Contents

Preface

*As far as we can discern, the sole purpose of human existence
is to kindle a light in the darkness of mere being.*
C.G. Jung, Erinnerungen, Traüme, Gedunken (1962).

Success in life is something that we should all hope for, and in a truly equitable world, we should all be able to achieve some reasonable measure of success in some aspects of our lives.

This book attempts to offer some insights into how to increase our chances of success in life.

Part I, Personal Life and Attributes, discusses how we should PLAN for success, have self-confidence and hope, have a sensible lifestyle (for example, not becoming 'brainwashed' *consumer zombies*), should avoid conflict as far as possible, look after our health with a healthy lifestyle, and have a positive attitude.

Part II, Lifelong Learning, discusses how we should continue to learn and gain new knowledge and skills throughout life, how home-based learning can help us do this, how effective study habits improve the results of such learning, how creativity and later learning increase *Real IQ*, and thinking and planning technique that may improve our chances of success in life.

Part III, The Workplace, discusses how the corporate workplace operates, leadership, how hierarchical organizations result in excessive advantage to those at the top, how to deal with 'bad bosses', and 'person scaling' to evaluate such bad bosses and other people in the workplace, perhaps including oneself for comparative purposes.

Part IV, Home Life, discusses how to find an appropriate partner in life, family planning, how to make a marriage work well, and how to raise smarter children more likely to succeed in life.

Part V, Social Life, discusses social activities which may be used for both recreational, health, and networking purposes, the usual formal structure for meetings (for example of local branches of political parties), and networking which is, of course, can help one be more successful in life.

Part VI, Conclusions, discusses several key ways in which we can improve our lives, the last chapter adding a few final points, including the 10th law of the new religion Mohronism, Mohr's Metrology, which is that, rather than judge many things in life as simply 'black or white', or 'good or bad', we should judge them on the Mohr Scale of 1 to 9 (for further information on Mohronism read *World Religions* by G.A. Mohr & Edwin Fear (2015), or *World Religions* by G.A., P.E. & R.S. Mohr (2018).

We hope some of the information contained in this book, some of which is new, proves helpful in readers make their lives happier and more successful.

Finally, once again I am grateful to the publishers for yet again doing an excellent job of promptly publishing this book.

Geoff Mohr
Melbourne, 2018

PART I
PERSONAL LIFE AND ATTRIBUTES

Chapter 1

PLANNING FOR SUCCESS

*Planning is as natural to the process of success
as its absence is to the process of failure.*
Robin Seiger, *Natural Born Winners* (1999).

Introduction

All too many of us go through life without sufficient planning, in part because we grow up with our lives largely controlled by parents and educators. Even at a young age, however, we should acquire the habit of planning our lives, at least in part, for example planning weekend activities with friends, and joining in planning of family activities.

In adult life, of course, planning is very important, for example planning personal and family activities and finances. We should also plan our working lives as far as possible, including in such plans our goals and aspirations, for example for better pay or a better job.

The following chapter gives examples of some of the common tools that can be used for planning, beginning with creative thinking to come up with ideas and goals for which we can then make plans.

Creative thinking

Divergent thinking involves considering a number of alternatives, some of which may be new and/or impractical, rather than seeking a single logical solution.

Creative thinking involves finding novel but practical solutions to a problem or task using divergent thinking and may occur in three stages (Morgan et al., 1979):

[1] Preparation: define the facts and materials needed for the new solution.

[2] Incubation: acquire further information, think about, and 'sleep on' the problem.

{3] Assembly: combine information to find the solution.

Creativity may be enhanced by 'undirected' or *autistic thinking*, as occurs in dreams, in which one's own 'personal' and unique concepts are freely associated. This is accomplished by *brainstorming* in which the mind is allowed to roam freely through as many ideas as possible.

Creative people enjoy creating things, are assertive, have a risk taking approach, tend to be impulsive, dislike constraints, like a little complexity, are objective about their efforts (i.e., able to critically examine them), and accept feedback from others.

Among other characteristics, creative people may also be intuitive, perceptive, ingenious, industrious, persistent, independent, unconventional, courageous, uninhibited, moody, self-centred and eccentric.

In conclusion: *"- - creativity is central to a rich, meaningful life"* (Butler-Bowdon, 2017a). More important, it is a key component of *real IQ* (Mohr, Sinclair & Fear, 2017).

Sometimes *brainstorming* helps solve a problem, and group brainstorming has been found effective because:

[1] People tend to have twice as many ideas in the group situation because of the more stimulating environment, 'cross fertilization' of ideas and arousal of competitive spirit.

[2] Alternation of individual and group thinking improves results.

[3] As more ideas are produced they tend to improve.

[4] Second sessions a few days later improve results because of the 'incubation' process so important in creative thinking.

[5] The group uses *critical thinking* to evaluate the ideas.

Problem solving

Problems can be attacked in three stages:

[1] Defining the problem
At first this might involve realizing that a problem exists.
Then we need to determine:
(a) What is the initial situation, i.e., what is known about the problem?
(b) What is the goal?
(c) What are the restrictions or *constraints*?
(d) What moves or *operations* are required to reach the goal?

[2] Generating possible solutions
Solutions to a problem can be obtained by such *strategies* as:

(a) In the case of mathematics problems, for example, *algorithms* can be used to try large numbers of solutions on a computer.

(b) Use an existing *heuristic rule* or 'rule of thumb.'

(c) Redefine the problem, for example by breaking it down into stages and seeking a 'solution' for each stage. Such *means-end analysis* is sometimes more successful if the problem is examined by working backwards through these stages.

(d) Use a new arrangement of existing techniques or materials.

(e) Invent new techniques or materials, i.e., use *insight learning*. This requires *creative thinking* which, as described earlier, often involves *incubation* periods.

Creative thinking can be inhibited by:

(i) *Functional fixedness,* the difficulty of imagining new uses for materials or devices.

(ii) *Mental set,* the difficulty in finding new strategies for approaching a problem. Mental set can be induced by recent experiences or old habits.

[3] Testing and evaluating the solutions

Alternative solutions are tested to see how well they work in relation to predetermined criteria.

Sometimes problems can be solved by *trial and error* so that trial solutions are repetitively adjusted until satisfactory.

Selection of the best solution from a number of alternatives should be done with a quantitative basis.

Lateral thinking

Edward de Bono proposed lateral thinking as an alternative to logical or *vertical* thinking. Some of the features of lateral thinking are:

➢ Steps can be jumped (and 'filled' later).

➢ Steps need not be 'correct' so long as the conclusion is correct and may be made in order to *generate* a new direction or branch.

➢ Interpretation of task criteria and alternative solution properties can be changed and the process is not *finite,* that is it need not reach a conclusion in any given time.

➢ It is *probabilistic* so that less obvious solutions are considered so that the best solution is obtained (if a valid solution exists).

De Bono (1982) recommends use of the word PO:

"PO is the laxative of language"

as an alternative to the words 'yes' and 'no' to emphasize that lateral thinking is not quick to say no to less obvious solutions and, rather than stop at obstacles to a solution, one should *go around* them by such means as those summarized above.

Whilst 'po' seems a somewhat trivial, if not absurd, idea, it may have some merit for many of us do indeed have a tendency to persist trying to solve some problems rather than 'go around' them.

Selecting the best candidate for a job is a good example. If this is done with lateral thinking:

[1] Some criteria might be ignored or downgraded in importance so that more candidates will be considered.

[2] Those that do not satisfy some criteria might remain under consideration.

[3] Candidates not at the top of the list are re-evaluated.

Lateral thinking is better understood with reference to the decision trees described in a later section. In these lateral thinking might encourage us to consider branches that have lower probabilities of success.

The bottom line, however, is that lateral thinking simply involves considering more than one possible solution to a problem or task.

In this context the first author uses the term 'bilemma' when one has difficulty deciding between two alternatives, and then the term 'trilemma' when there are three alternatives, viewing the latter as the preferred situation as he feels it fairly easy to knock out one of three alternatives.

Worrying

Earlier, three stages of creative thinking were mentioned, the second of these being *incubation*.

This implies a somewhat relaxed way of approaching things. In fact *worrying* about problems is a key part of how many people try to solve them.

Indeed, people with a habit of developing ideas over the long term tend also to suffer some degree of anxiety over them, regularly worrying about how to improve them and find a final solution.

Newton, for example, used to awake with an idea and spend hours at his bedside getting it down on paper. Not surprisingly, he had three nervous breakdowns at Cambridge University, leaving at the age of 42.

Perhaps Thomas Alva Edison, with 1093 patents to his name, perhaps thanks to a few years of home schooling, is a better example, having developed the habit of inventing things at an early age (Heyn, 1976).

Worrying about a problem might take place in various ways, for example:

[1] Tossing and turning in your sleep or walking the streets.

[2] Subconsciously worrying about them and perhaps waking at the end of an REM sleep phase with a possible answer.

[3] Writing notes about the problem, adding to these when additional ideas arise.

[4] Looking up books and asking other people to try and find the answer.

[5] Making a note of the problem somewhere such as in a diary or on the corner of a notice board.

As we must all have experienced sometimes, however, if we worry about the problem long enough we eventually see it a little more clearly and often come up with an answer.

Mohr's laws of decisions

Essentially, the major problem of the human race is the habit of making bad decisions.

Some of us, at least, are very good at creative thinking to produce new ideas and products, and others are good at making the things we most need such as food, clothing and shelter.

As a result of the devastatingly accurate Peter Principle, all too many of our leaders and managers are, more often than not, guilty of bad decisions, if not corruption.

If a leader commits us to an unjustified war then, just as architects do, he praises his mistake. If a worker makes a small error or two he is dismissed.

Self-evident as they may be, Mohr's Laws of Decisions (Mohr, 2014b, 2018d) are some help:

1) Don't rush.

2) Don't take the first offer or run with the first idea.

3) Look for alternative ideas and build an ideas/options list.

4) List the requirements or inputs for each option.

5) List the results or outputs for each option.

6) Calculate the ratio of the outputs to inputs for each option.

7) Double check the accuracy of 4 - 6.

8) Select the option with the highest output/input ratio.

9) Ask at least a second opinion.

10) Sleep on it.

The analysis of steps 4 - 6 corresponds to *cost-benefit* analysis, a simple technique widely used in economic studies of infrastructure and other plans to decide on the best program of work.

Many a housewife probably uses a somewhat similar decision making approach but the usually moronic politicians who run countries find such stuff hard going and have to employ thousands of economists and statisticians to perform these rudimentary analyses.

Needless to say they usually get it wrong, often when somebody's palm is greased, for example by a construction company seeking the contract for a major government project.

Decision tables

A good example is the following table of the performance of three categories of stocks and shares under boom, steady and slump market conditions.

	Boom (a)	Steady (b)	Slump (c)
Gilt edged (x)	5 %	5	5
Speculative (y)	20	0	-10
Unit trusts (z)	10	5	0

What then is the best mix of shares to buy?

The *deterministic solution* is as follows. For a 10 year cycle time in business conditions assume $a = 1$, $b = 6$ and $c = 3$ years. Then the profit (%) from each of the three share types is:

$$x:\ 5 + 30 + 15 = 50$$
$$y:\ 20 - 30 = -10$$
$$z:\ 10 + 30 = 40$$

so that one should buy x or z but not y (unless boom conditions are assured for a known period).

Decision trees

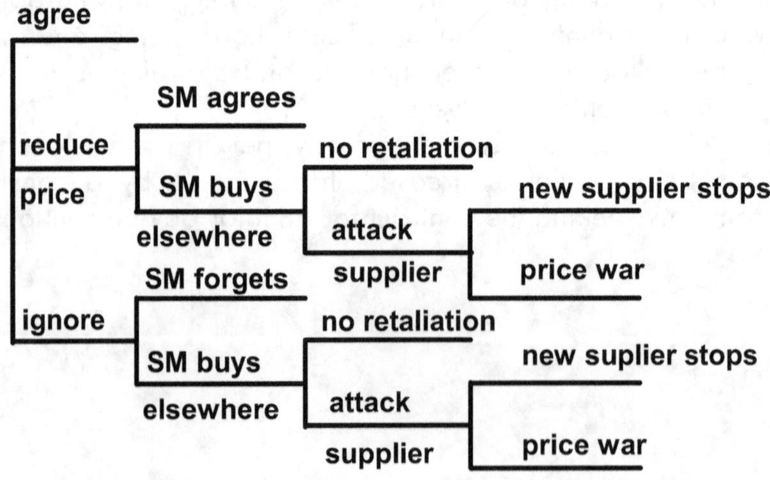

Figure 14.1. Example of a decision tree.

Decision trees are a useful way of depicting business strategies. A simple example is that of a manufacturer asked by a supermarket chain to make a 'home brand' version of its product, a decision tree for which is shown in Figure 14.1.

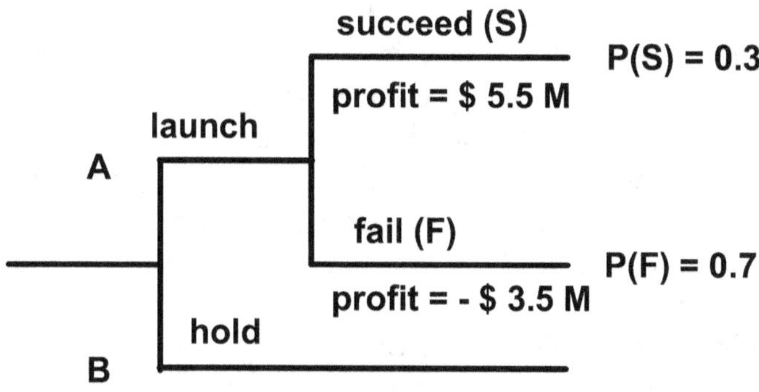

Figure 14.2. Decision tree with probabilities and financial outcomes.

As another example Figure 14.2 considers the problem of deciding whether to launch a rocket at a certain time or not, attaching probabilities and profit figures to the decision tree.

Then the Expected Monetary Value (EMV) of a launch is 0.3(5.5) - 0.7(3.5) = - \$0.8M so we should decide to hold.

With more optimistic figures, for example P(S) = 0.7 and P(F) = 0.3, the EMV of **A** is \$2.85M and the launch decision is much more favourable, though perhaps still not certain.

Conclusion

Decision trees, especially if they have probabilities and costs attached, are useful tools in the decision making process.

Decision tables are also useful, especially if they have weighted quantities to enable a total score to be given to the alternatives under consideration.

Mohr's Laws of Decisions are for the most part rudimentary, but nonetheless worth note. 'Don't rush', for example is very important and the basis of the cliché:

Err in haste, repent at leisure.

Similarly, getting a second (if not more) opinion and 'sleeping on it' are, of course, important. Board meetings of most organizations, for example, are typically monthly and run for two or three hours. Sometimes, however, there may be a long agenda and/or some important issues that require prolonged discussion and debate, and discussion of unresolved issues must be adjourned to a special meeting, or the next regular meeting.

In dealing with enthusiastic and 'pushy' sales persons, for example, one must be very careful, and trying to sell or buy a house can be a nightmare for 'ordinary' people. Auctions, in particular, cruelly force first home buyers to compete with experienced investors in a ridiculously hasty 'sidewalk show', often pressuring them into paying too high a price.

In such situations, of course, they need to have planned carefully in what area they want to live, how much they can afford to pay, what is a fair price they can limit themselves to paying, of course getting as much advice from friends or independent professional advisors as possible.

Chapter 2

BUILDING SELF-CONFIDENCE AND HOPE

He who does not hope to win has already lost.
José Juaquin Olmedo, (1780-1847), attrib.

Hope against hope, and ask till ye receive.
James Montgomery, "The World Before the Flood",
The Poetical Works of James Montgomery (1840-41).

Self-esteem and self-confidence

Some psychologists argue that self-esteem has two components: *self-efficacy* and *self-respect* (Krapp, 2005), and in order to increase self-belief often counsel patients to:
   (a) Repeat to themselves such statements of affirmation as: *"I believe in myself"* to increase self-belief.
   (b) Associate with positive people to obtain encouragement and support.
   (c) List their past successes and review this list periodically to increase their levels of optimism.

Dr Robert Anthony in his 2010 book *The Ultimate Secrets of Total Self-Confidence* describes a "simple but very effective learning technique" in which over a period of only 21 days patients "break an old destructive habit and form a new positive one." Various chapters encourage readers to:
   ➢ "Dehypnotise" themselves.
   ➢ Develop self-reliance.
   ➢ Think positively.
   ➢ Use "creative imagination".
   ➢ Develop a "direct action worksheet".
   ➢ "Get the smile habit".

The final chapter concludes that a positive mental attitude gives a person self-confidence.

It could also be added, of course, that a positive attitude givens one hope, and with hope comes some degree of confidence.

Self-regulation

Bandura's social-cognitive theory holds that people are capable of self-regulation and thus controlling their own behaviour, and that the self-regulation process has three parts (Krapp, 2005):

[1] Self-observation: tracking one's own thoughts, feelings and behaviours.

[2] Judgment: comparing oneself to standards set by oneself or, preferably, others.

[3] Self-response: rewarding oneself for doing well and punishing oneself for doing badly.

For example, a student doing poorly at mathematics can self-regulate their performance by (Krapp, 2005):

[1] Write down their negative thoughts associated with maths classes, homework, and tests.

[2] Set a realistic goal for improvement, for example if the student is getting C grades, they should be somewhat optimistic and aim for B grades, not C+ as this is not a sufficiently rewarding goal, and not A+ as this is not a realistic goal.

[3] Note but not dwell too much on any lack of improvement, but celebrate improvement when it comes.

Self-assessment

Sensible and accurate self-assessment is, of course, very important throughout life, and this should include several of the key facets of one's life, and Table 2.1 is an example 'life-assessment' for a married person in their mid-30s with a job and two children.

Table 2.1. Self-assessment for married person.

Factor	Present situation	Score/10
Job	OK	6
Marriage	OK	7
Family finances	?	5
Home life	Good	8
Child 1	Problems	4
Child 2	Good	8
House	OK	7
Car	Old	6
Social life	Very little	3
Total score/100		**54**

The total score is mediocre, to say the least, and perhaps a better job could be hoped for to improve it, and thence the family finances and situation in general.

If weights were added to each factor, as in the Expectancy-Value and Information Integration models of attitude formation discussed in Chapter 6, then a better assessment is obtained. A relatively high weight would be given to the 'job' factor, of course, as this affects most, if not all, of the other 9 factors.

In the case of a school-age child, of course, the factors would by very different, including marks at school, friends, extra-curricular activities such as sports, 'pocket money', and perhaps food as children, of course, have to do as they are told on most things, including what they eat, and their earliest signs of discontent are often diet-related.

Social support

When things go wrong it is, of course, helpful to have supportive people, whether they be relatives, friends, or counselors, to turn to for advice and moral support.

Such people can provide help and encouragement that may provide hope in the most difficult of circumstances, and hope alone in most cases will help one cope in the short term.

Then, in the longer term, one can begin to fix the problem(s) in question, or 'move on' from them to work towards new goals.

Successful businesswoman Lillian Vernon recalls: *My father told me I had talent and a good idea for starting a business and I should never let anything get in the way of fulfilling my dream, or I would regret it for the rest of my life*, concluding: *So don't let challenges, setbacks, or detractors defeat or discourage you. If you believe in yourself and think positively, you will succeed* (Trump, 2004).

Hope improves life

A home-based study of almost 800 people included the simple question:

Are you hopeful about the future?

Regardless of their sex or ethnicity, 91% of the respondents replied "yes", the other 9% replying "no" (Lopez, 2013).

The two groups, the "hopeful" and the "hopeless", were almost the same age (averaging respectively 69 and 70), had the same levels of education and health, with "no significant differences in blood pressure, body mass index, and drinking behaviour".

The hopeful, however, had higher levels of physical activity, fewer were smokers, tested for much lower levels of depression and higher measures of social well-being, had more social contacts, and were slightly better off financially.

About a decade later only 11% of the hopefuls had died, compared to 29% of the hopeless, the principal researcher concluding that: "If you are hopeless you are less likely to keep doctor's appointments" (Lopez, 2013).

Hope vs. optimism

The 2nd edition of the Macquarie Dictionary defines hope as: 1. expectation of something desired; desire accompanied by expectation.

2. a particular instance of such expectation or desire: *a hope of success.*

It defines optimism as:

1. disposition to hope for the best; tendency to look on the bright side of things.

while defining optimistic as:

1. Disposed to take a favourable view of things.

Here optimism is a mood, a state of mind, usually without a specific goal, whereas hope is usually associated with a particular wish or ambition.

According to Lopez, however, hope is more important:

But when life throws us a curve, when the going gets tough, optimists get stuck and frustrated. Hopeful people shine in negative situations. They are energized to act and they find meaning and dignity in moving ahead, whatever the challenge.

Creating goals

In his 1994 book *The Psychology of Hope,* Charles Snyder postulates that hope has three key elements:

1. The ability to envision goals.
2. The understanding that there are alternative pathways to a goal.
3. Self-efficacy, that is, the capacity to muster up power and energy in pursuit of that goal.

Happy and successful lives are far more likely if we plan them by creating goals. These should be realistic in terms of time and resource requirements, and goals which we are enthusiastic about are, of course, more likely to receive attention and thus be achieved.

When a goal involves solving a problem it is best to think positively about it. If one is having problems with a co-worker Jim, for example, rather than think:

I want to have less trouble with Jim

it is better to think: *I want to make friends with Jim*

and act positively by, for example, paying him polite compliments occasionally.

It is also best, of course, to choose goals that your abilities are best suited to, and Chapter 1 detailed some systematic methods of planning for a successful life.

Motivation

Aristotle was first to assert that our goal was to become more nearly what we were intended to be. Psychologists refer to this is as *self-actualization* and Maslow viewed this as striving to reach our potential (Lindzey at al., 1978). He defined two kinds of needs:

(a) *Basic needs* such as hunger, thirst, sex and security.

(b) *Metaneeds* such as achievement, beauty, goodness, justice, order and unity.

Maslow defined achievement as a basic need but the present author prefers to classify it as a 'higher' or more human metaneed.

First, we must meet our basic or 'animal' needs. That done, we can turn our attention to the higher 'human' metaneeds, and thence self-actualization as a human being.

These needs provide *primary goals* that may motivate us towards *secondary goals* such as money in order to achieve them.

Most of our basic needs are *intrinsic motivations*. Of these, *competence motivation* is perhaps the most basic and is learnt by infants challenged by goals such as standing up in their cot or walking.

Most of our metaneeds are *learned goals*. Achievement motivation, for example, can be inculcated by parents or teachers. *Social motivations* such as justice are also acquired in this way.

What has this got to do with thinking? One's motivations will, of course, greatly influence how one thinks and acts.

Some studies have found, however, little correlation between motivation and efficiency of learning, suggesting that genetics and practice are more important factors.

Mindset

Psychologist Carol Dweck in her 2006 book *Mindset: The New Psychology of Success,* made the important distinction between:

(a) *Fixed mindset* which focuses heavily upon outcome: "If you fail – or if you're not the best – it's all been wasted."

(b) *Growth mindset* which focuses more upon the effort and what might have been learnt from it.

According to Butler-Bowdon some fixed mindset people allow a poor result in a single test, such as for IQ, to limit their ambitions and efforts for the rest of their lives (Butler-Bowden, 2017a).

Growth mindset people, on the other hand, think much more positively and aim for new and higher goals with the view that, no matter what the outcome, they will at least have tried or 'given it a go', and can learn from the effort and thus hope to do better next time.

In a study of university students, Dweck found that those with fixed mindsets had higher levels of depression and were more likely to give up when their results were poor. Students with a growth mindset with poor results, however, took the more positive view that they had made some progress, and increased their efforts in order to obtain better results.

Leading with hope

Lopez (2013) cites a telephone Gallup poll of more than 10,000 people which asked them what three words best described how bosses or community leaders contributed positively to their life. It turned out that words such as *wisdom* were rarely mentioned, but that respondents said *"they want the people they serve to meet four psychological needs: compassion, stability, trust, and hope."*

Lopez concludes that most leaders *"do not spend enough time making hope happen"* but spend more time reacting to problems rather than planning for a better future.

The Gallup poll found that 69% of people who said their workplace leader make them enthusiastic about the future rated highly on measures of their involvement with and enthusiasm for their work. They were also more innovative, productive, and likely to stay longer with the company.

On the other hand, only 1% of those who did not find their boss made them enthusiastic about the future were committed to and enthusiastic about their work. They were also likely to be physically and mentally unhealthy, and to undermine the work of others.

Teacher expectancy effect

The teacher expectancy effect is based on the observation that students aware of the fact that the teacher considers them 'bright' tend to do better than they otherwise would, even if they are not actually exceptional. In addition, teachers tend to mark students they consider bright more favourably. Thus we have a double barreled effect.

For the present discussion, however, we shall merely consider an *expectancy effect* for which we write

$$\text{Motivation} = (\text{Valence}) \times (\text{Expectancy})$$

where *valence* is the desire for marks (or in other spheres for $) and *expectancy* is the person's notion of the probability of obtaining a certain mark (perhaps enhanced by the teacher or, just as likely, by knowledge of their own record).

This expectancy is of a first level outcome (obtaining certain marks) with a second level outcome expected to follow from the first outcome (such as approval by parents).

This theory emphasizes the different levels of motivation that will exist in different people and managers should, if possible, have some idea of the motivation of their staff and, in addition, make some effort to enhance this by increasing their expectancy.

Things we hope for

There are many things people hope for in life, some of the key ones being:

➢ Good marks at school.
➢ To do well at sports.
➢ To get a good job.
➢ To make money.
➢ To own a house.
➢ To find love and marriage.
➢ To have children.
➢ To be healthy.
➢ To be content, if not happy, with life.
➢ To have a long life.

There are many less important things we hope for, of course, including that our favourable sporting team wins, that the weather will be nice, to have a nice outing at the weekend, to have a holiday before long, etcetera.

A major issue, of course, is how we deal with disappointment when are hopes are not realized.

When this happens we should consider whether the hope in question was realistic. If on further consideration we believe it was realistic/achievable, then we should:

➢ Extend the timeframe for achieving the goal.
➢ Consider alternative means of achieving it.
➢ Consider getting help to achieve it.

and examples of the sorts of decision making processes that might be employed are given in Chapter 11.

When things go wrong

There are many bad things that can happen in life, some of which can be most upsetting, for example:

➢ Getting bad marks at school.
➢ Failing and having to repeat a year at school.
➢ Losing a job.
➢ Marriage and family breakdown.
➢ Psychological problems.

> Physical health problems.
> Financial problems.
> Excessive use of, and addiction to alcohol or drugs.

When one has such problems one should always seek advice and help from family, friends, and professional to think difficult situations through and find solutions to them.

In the case of physical health problems, of course, one's GP should be the first port of call, whereas for problems at school teachers should be consulted. Family and friends may be able to help deal with minor psychological problems, but for major ones professional help should be sought.

For married couples with children, the 'breadwinner' losing his or her job can be a major catastrophe, of course, one that often leads to marriage and family break-up.

Whilst marriage counselors often help with marital difficulties, finding a 'good' job can be very difficult, especially when one has been unemployed for a substantial period of time, in part because answering questions at interview such as: "What are you doing now?" honestly will greatly reduce one's prospects, especially if reference statements from previous employers are not highly supportive.

Indeed, in such situations, one really needs a credible advocate or supporter to accompany one to the interview for support and to help plead one's case.

Conclusions

For best results one must, of course, tackle life and its occasional problems with the inter-related personal characteristics and behaviours:
> Self-esteem.
> Self-confidence.
> Self-reliance.
> Self-belief.
> Focus on main goals.
> Self-regulation or control.
> Self-assessment in similar fashion to the Information Integration model of attitude formation (see Chapter 6).

> ➤ Realistic goal-setting.
> ➤ Support from friends etc. with problems, and in achieving one's goals.

Then, if one has self-confidence, achievable goals etc., one also has HOPE without which, of course, life can be unbearable.

Chapter 3

SENSIBLE LIFESTYLE

*The idea that the media is there to educate us, or to inform us,
is ridiculous because that's about tenth or eleventh on their list.
The first purpose of the media is to sell us shit.*
Abbie Hoffman, speech at U South Carolina (September 16, 1987).

*A habit cannot be tossed out the window,
it must be coaxed down the stairs one step at a time.*
Mark Twain, attributed.

Introduction

Those who have a 'good', sensible, productive etc. lifestyle are far more likely to be successful in life. Such people will give have life-improving goals and work hard to achieve those goals, giving themselves plenty of thinking time to deal with any problems that might arise, and getting help from friends, workmates, professional advisors etc. to make sure their goals are achieved.

It is also important, of course, to avoid becoming a brainwashed 'consumer zombie' and become addicted to such bad and expensive habits as gambling, smoking, excessive booze consumption, or other extravagant habits such as needlessly expensive clothes, cars etc.

Hoping to help readers avoid becoming consumer zombies, the psychology of advertising is briefly discussed in following sections.

The purpose of advertising

Nowadays, of course, there are massive media and advertising industries devoted to turning us into consumer zombies.

The main objectives of ads, in approximate order of priority, are to:

1. Make the brand name familiar.
2. To give the brand a distinct image.
3. Attribute at least one key attribute to that brand name.
4. Associate the product with certain usages.
5. To convince us that this brand is the best (for us).
6. To persuade us that we should buy the product.

To meet these objectives ads will involve:

slogans, demonstrations, comparisons, testimonials, and repetition.

Comparisons, of course, are usually of price, but sometimes also some sort of semi-official rating, for example safety ratings for cars.

By way of style ad types include basic facts, 'mood', feel-good, social setting, slice-of-life, humour, fantasy, hard-sell, and anxiety/danger/risk or 'fear' ads.

The psychology of attitudes

Attitude can be defined as 'psychological *tendency* expressed by *evaluating* a particular entity with some degree of favour or disfavour.'

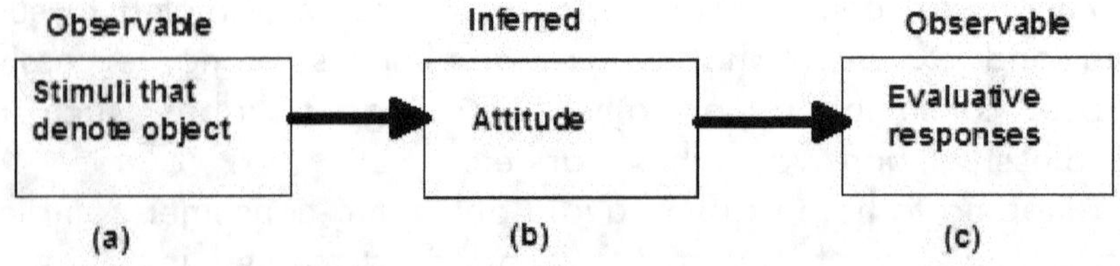

Figure 3.1. Psychological responses

Figure 3.1 illustrates the three types of response involved in attitudinal psychology.

These are:

1. *Cognitive response.* This response is that of recognition of, for example, a name, a picture or other stimulus.

2. *Affective response.* This is a hypothetical construct and a latent variable. Here the sympathetic nervous system responds to (1) with feelings or emotions.

3. *Behavioural response.* This is the outward expression of (2) and may be a positive, neutral or negative response of some degree or intensity involving some observable action.

In this context, for example, conservatism, environmentalism or racism are objects. Then when we label a person a conservative, environmentalist or racist we infer an attitudinal position. Such attitudes are evidenced and also developed by the *'CAB* 'mechanism illustrated in Figure 3.1.

Schemas

Schemas are cognitive structures that represent a person's past experience in a stimulus domain by a higher order or abstract cognitive structure. Then attitude is a subset of such a schema.

Schemas have a selective effect on the retention, retrieval and remembering of information so that people have a better remembrance of stimuli that 'fit' their schemas and also for those that 'oppose.' This same selectivity applies to the 'input' of information as well as its output.

Functions of attitudes

Attitudes are necessary as part of our information processing system and have the following functions:

1. Knowledge function. Attitudes play an important role in summarizing past experience.

2. Adjustment or 'utilitarian' function. This proposed function has its roots in learning theory and enables people to maximize rewards in their environment and minimize punishment or losses.

3. Ego-defensive function. This has its roots in the idea of a defence mechanism and involves trying to avoid unpleasant realities.

4. Value-expressive function. This is related to the concept of the ego and social psychology and involves the expression of personal values and self-concept through attitude formation.

It follows from this theory that people like, and hence are motivated, to organize and simplify stimuli and collate related cognitions. Thus attitudes themselves energize and direct behaviour, that is, they motivate action as well as determine the form of reactions.

The reception-yielding model

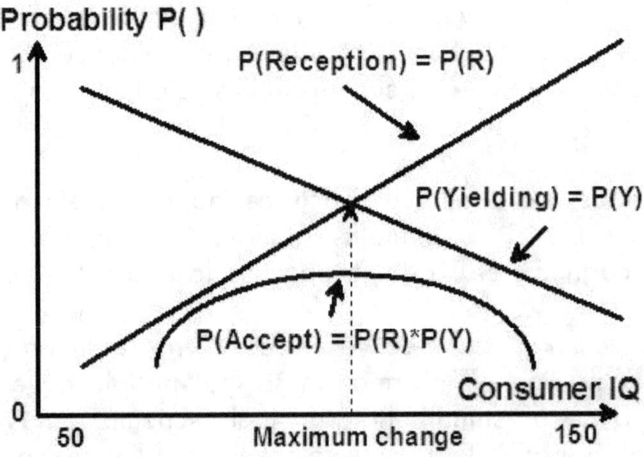

Figure 3.2. Probability of reception, yielding & attitude change.

Of particular importance is McGuire's reception-yielding model of attitude formation shown in Figure 3.2 (Eagly & Chaiken, 1993). Here 'reception' refers to comprehending a 'message', for example an advertisement. This model postulates that the probability of attitude change is given by:

$$P(C) = P(R) \times P(Y)$$

so that a maximum change is obtained where the reception and yielding curves intersect, as shown in Figure 3.2.

One application of this idea is to 'get them young' so that advertising companies target the young and naive before they have the maturity or 'consumer intelligence' to develop resistance. Thus, once an idea like 'beer is for the men' is buried in a boy's brain he may become a beer drinker for life, the habit occasionally reinforced by ads that make the habit look completely appropriate.

An excellent example of this was given by Sir Edgar Saunders addressing the Brewer's Society in Birmingham in 1930 (Sargent, 1979):

The chief customers of the public house today are the elderly and middle-aged men. Unless you can attract the younger generation to take the place of the older men, there is no doubt that we shall have to face a steadily falling consumption . . . if we begin advertising in the press we shall see the continuance of our advertising is contingent upon the fact that we get educational support as well in the same papers.

In that way it is wonderful how you can educate public opinion, generally, without making it too obvious that there is a public campaign behind it all.

The basic mechanism of persuasion, therefore, is to 'get them young' (and naive or 'less intelligent consumers') as Figure 3.2 suggests. To do this ads need only persuade/brainwash some of the target audience and then imitative or 'social' learning ensures that many of the rest follow them.

Advertisements having achieved this, regular advertising reminds the audience of a product. Then in Figure 3.1 the 'C' response will be one of recognition of your brand, the 'A' response will be one of approval of it, and the 'B' response will be to make a mental note to buy it.

The forgetting curves of Figure 3.3 have important application in developing long term marketing plans. Here curves A and B are for two messages and curve B* is the result after the second message is repeated.

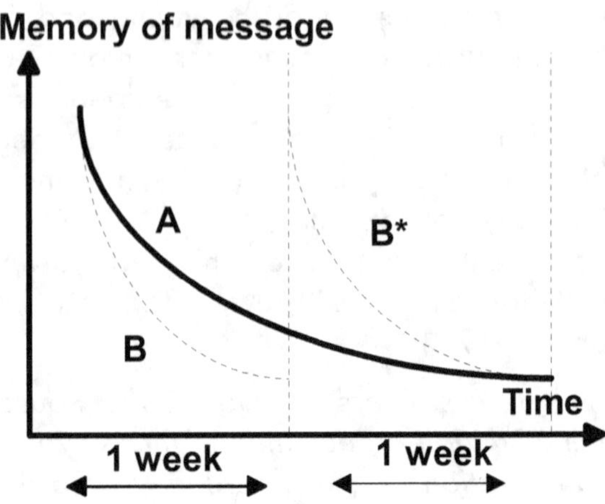

Figure 3.3. Forgetting curves.

Then, after time has elapsed after an advertisement, its 'residual' effect depends upon both the *primacy*, or strength of the ad compared to others, and its *recency*. In Figure 3.3, after two weeks ad B* has greater recency than ad A, but less primacy so that they have nearly equal effect.

In such studies, however, correlation between retention and persuasion is by no means guaranteed.

Targeting advertising

Maslow's two kinds of needs, *basic needs* and *metaneeds,* were discussed in the preceding chapter.

Advertising usually targets the metaneeds of the *ego.*

A Coke ad, for example, is not designed to remind you that you may be thirsty. If so, you might rush to the fridge and grab whatever drink you can find to satisfy that thirst. No, a Coke ad makes it look 'cool' to drink Coke with your friends and being 'cool' is a metaneed! So next day a young boy will want to be 'cool' when hanging out with his friends so they will all drink Coke and act foolishly, just like the actors in the Coke ads

Here again we see the down side of advertising, namely that increasingly ambitious executives will stop at nothing to sell their product, even if it has to brainwash the young into acquiring both bad behaviour and bad teeth.

In marketing to children, of course, familiar cuddly looking cartoon figures are often displayed on packaging and used to speak the lines of TV ads. Here, however, ads usually target the *Id,* the basic 'animal' personality that has basic needs like hunger. Young children tend to eat in smaller doses and often so that almost any time they are awake is a good one to put a picture of confectionery in front of them.

One of the best examples of brainwashing, however, is the use of *consumer panels* of children in marketing research. The children are often asked what they will say and do to persuade parents to buy them the product.

Finally, the extent to which children are exposed to advertising is incredible:

- - *"it is estimated that children between two and 11 years old may see over 20,000 advertisements in a year,"*
(O'Guinn et al., 2006).

Advertising, therefore, will brainwash someone in your family, even if it doesn't brainwash you!

Push and pull marketing

Some marketing campaigns use *push strategies* which concentrate on the availability of products. In this case the ads are 'basic' and concentrate on telling you the product name and where to get it. Examples of such ads on TV are
➤ A presenter reads a script while holding the product in question up in front of the camera.
➤ Ads with only text messages and a voice-over.
➤ Semi-humorous ads which sometimes use cartoon characters to present their message.
➤ Ads targeting children which involve cuddly characters and fantasy scenes and the like.
➤ Ads for junk food which play on having a high 'reward/effort' ratio (Govoni et al., 1988). That 50 million

people a day eat McDonald's stuff is testament enough to the success of their advertising.

➤ Ads where the reader just about screams at you not to miss some bargain sale or to go to some cheap store.

Advertisements for 'basic' food, junk food, confectionery, clothing and home appliances are usually of the 'push' type.

Marketing campaigns often use *pull strategies* which promote the product in order to attract buyers. In this case the ads concentrate on 'image' to attract the audience to the product and the product name is secondary and *associated* with the imagery. Examples of this sort of ad on TV are:

➤ Sophisticated ads that show the product in 'classy' surroundings with actors dressed stylishly.

➤ "Laid back' ads were the presenter extols the virtue of the product with, for example, an island resort as a backdrop.

➤ Ads that use glamorous people such as movie stars as actors.

This type of advertising is usually used for higher priced or more 'up market' products, including fashion clothing, cosmetics, expensive furniture, luxury cars and overseas holidays.

One of the most important 'levers' in advertising, undoubtedly, is *keeping up with the Jones's*. This is exploited heavily in marketing cars and new gadgets of which the mobile phone is the supreme example at present.

Another powerful inducement is selling on the 'never-never', for example with no repayments for a year.

The ubiquitousness of advertising

Today advertising is literally everywhere. On TV in Australia there used to be regulations limiting the amount of advertisements per hour to something bearable. Now there seem like 20 minutes or more of ads per hour at times. Worse still, owing to the increasing cost of TV advertising time a truly bewildering string of ads appears in each ad break, sometimes dozen of them.

It is almost as bad on radio where there are sometimes as many as half a dozen ads at once on the higher rating commercial stations.

Junk mail from supermarkets and other retail chains has reached epidemic proportions. Other 'direct marketing' is done by phone and is increasingly irritating, often involving requests to complete lengthy market research surveys over the phone.

In addition, free local papers almost totally full of advertisements are also stuffed into millions of letterboxes in major cities.

Trams, trains and buses carry plenty of ads, as do train stations and tram and bus stops. Taxis and trucks all carry signage, as do many vehicles belonging to small businesses.

Shopping strips are becoming more and more cluttered with advertising signs above the shops, and sandwich boards and often products on the footpath.

More and more restaurants, coffee shops and juice bars have also spilled out onto footpaths, sometimes making little room for the pedestrians for which they were originally intended.

Shopping malls are filled with advertising and more and more stalls with spruikers have appeared in them.

Sporting grounds carry more and more advertising and sporting teams now carry prominent advertising on their clothing.

Casual clothing often comes complete with the brand name writ large upon it.

The Internet is full of advertising, of course, some of it of a lurid nature.

Then there is the despicable practice of placing confectionery and soft drinks near the checkouts at supermarkets, resulting in many a tantrum as young children taken shopping throw a tantrum to get another dose of perhaps the first 'drug' of addiction, sugar.

Perhaps the most predatory advertiser of all, Coca Cola, has its vending machines just about everywhere, including pubs and clubs, take-away food shops, office buildings, stations and heaven knows where else.

A few simple marketing ploys

Most commonly, of course, every effort is made to make you focus on how much you are saving, not much how you are spending. Some of us can't resist a bargain and can't get wise to the fact that when you buy something you don't need discounted from $10 to $9, you have not saved a dollar, you have wasted $9.

One classical way of getting you to buy a brand of razor blades for the long term was to sell the razor cheaply or even give it away. This came to be known as the 'give away the razor and sell the blades approach' and was often associated with the Gillette company.

This approach is now used widely, for example cheap printers for PCs for which replacement ink cartridges cost almost as much as the original printer.

In selling electrical goods or furniture the 'interest free' lure is often used. This simply involves an appropriate boosting of the price of the goods being sold in this way.

A litany of lies

Advertising bullshit is often, of course, a pack of lies, a few examples being:

➢ Despite growing awareness of the need to limit dietary fat we are still encouraged to eat meat often and to consume products such as snack foods which are heavily laden with fat.

➢ Milk: the finding many years ago that milk has a protein believed responsible for autism was suppressed by the milk industry in New Zealand until recently. As a child the first author knew a doctor who believed one of his children had contracted polio in the 50s from milk, perhaps kept to the second day. Such news is always suppressed as it would be bad for business.

➢ In the 1950's and 1960's petrol was always advertised as having some new additive or other. Few, if any, of these had any effect and the industry knew this full well.

➢ Cigarettes The addictive and cancer producing effects of cigarettes were concealed far too long.

➢ Up to 15% of children in some parts of the USA are on drugs for newly 'invented' problems such as Attention Deficit Disorder (ADD). This so-called disease is simply an excuse for children who get low marks at school when this is 'unfashionable.' This is a practice that would have disturbed Hitler and Stalin.

Conclusion

Rather than become a consumer zombie, one should have sensible, productive habits aimed at achieving important life goals, including having a bearable job, making enough money to live reasonably well, looking after one's health, and having a happy family life.

Chapter 4

AVOIDING CONFLICT

*[The boss] told a woman she "should have been drowned at birth and
called another "porky", "wog" and a "big fat bush pig".
He threatened to dissolve employees in acid, told a woman
a rapist was "waiting for you" and said all women
were "dogs" who were "only good for one thing."*
Article by Steve Butcher, *The Age*, 6th December 2012.

Introduction

It is, of course, important to avoid conflict as far as possible throughout life. Bullying in schools and workplaces, however, remains a major problem in society, and can greatly affect victims, often ruining their lives. The following chapter briefly discusses Mohr's attitudinal model of conflict, focusing on bullying in the workplace, where it is most common, and where it is most likely to have a very negative effect on victims' lives.

Like bullying in schools, workplace bullying is also a big issue now, the foregoing quotation from a newspaper article being an extreme example of it that occurred in a small business.

Estimates of prevalence rates for workplace bullying in Australia range from 3.5% to 15% and according to Healey (2011): *About one in six people are bullied at work; in some industries the figure is higher, ranging from 25 percent, 50 percent to 97 percent.*

A survey of 5,300 employees in the UK found a prevalence rate of 10.5%, whilst a survey of the population of Michigan in the USA found a prevalence rate of a whopping 21.5%. At such a rate 1.5 million Australian employees would have been victims of bullying in 2000 with a cost to businesses of between 17 and 36 billion dollars (Healey, 2011).

An attitudinal model of conflict

A 'first approximation' formula for assessing the potential for conflict between a person or group assessed and another person or group was proposed by Mohr (Mohr, 2014a; Mohr et al., 2018c). With a slight modification, it takes the form:

$$A^* = A + xB + yC - zD + fS \tag{4.1}$$

where A^* = current 'overall' attitude,
A = initial or 'basic' attitude (based on 'known history'),
B = attitudes towards behaviours of the second party,
C = contact history between the two parties,
D = degree of difference between the parties considered,
S = 'societal attitude' towards the conflict,
and A, B, C, D and S may be positive or negative, negative values for D indicating 'similarity', rather than 'difference.'
and x, y, z, f are scaling factors that indicate the relative importance of the terms and here will be assumed unity for simplicity.

Equation 4.1 can, of course, be used to assess the attitude of both parties involved in the assessment.

Here attitude is assessed in the same way as attitude is measured by the information integration model of Equation 6.2 but for simplicity only scale values (but not weights) will be given to a small set of items in measuring A.

Similarly, only scale values are used in assessing B, C and D. These extra terms add a great deal to the 'basic' A assessment to give a 'picture' of the 'overall' attitude.

Application to workplace bullying

The components of Equation 4.1, that is:

Attitude $A^{**} = A + B + C - D + S$

have considerable relevance to workplace bullying:

[1] The **initial attitude A** of bullies is that they are superior, perhaps because they have a higher rank in the organizational hierarchy.

Their victims may be deemed to be inferior because they are smaller, weaker, of different race or gender, or simply new to the organization and thus have few friends in it as yet.

Highly competitive work environments can encourage bullying, the armed services being a well-known example:

Colleague: a competitor known to you by his first name, often working in your organization and vying with you for promotion and other perks (Marks et al., 2006).

[2] With greater confidence the bullying **behaviour** (**B**) is likely to grow worse over time, eventually requiring intervention in many cases.

Often, however, bullying affects the victim's workplace performance and their psychology. Indeed, the results can be serious, ranging from loss of promotion or job, to loss of career, divorce and suicide.

[3] Soon a negative **contact history** (**C**) builds up between the bully and the victim and the bully becomes increasingly confident if not opposed in any way.

[4] It is such **differences** (**D**) as rank, as noted in [1], that are the excuse for bullying. Bullies might also have type A personalities and thus be ambitious, driven and hostile.

[5] **Societal attitudes** (**S**) are now very strongly against workplace bullying to the point at which victims stand a much better chance of gaining help and support. Occasional media coverage of bullying is also helpful.

For example, an article in 'The Age' on 27/12/2012 entitled *Inquiry call on CSIRO 'bullying'* which reported that at a single site: "There may have been tens of claims of workplace bullying, intimidation and/or harassment, and other forms of misconduct that have not been fully or adequately investigated, and where a strong possibility exists that, at the very least, due process has been breached."

There have been many such articles in recent years, most of them about schools, and this repeated exposure of the issue has raised the level of public concern and helped instigate remedial actions in some schools and other organizations.

Bullying behaviours

There are five main types of workplace bullying:
➢ Work-related.
➢ Personal attacks.
➢ Social isolation
➢ Verbal threats.
➢ Rumour spreading.

Bullying behaviours can vary from easily noticed, aggressive and loud blaming and threats, to 'backstabbing' that damages the victim's reputation in the organization.

Usually the victim eventually suspects he or she is being backstabbed but is unsure of where the rumours are coming from, if not paranoid about it.

Usually bullying will involve both open aggression and covert backstabbing, the full range of behaviours being:

➢ Banter and teasing.
➢ Blame and verbal abuse.
➢ Personal abuse and humiliation.
➢ Yelling, screaming and offensive language.
➢ Professional denigration.
➢ Overt threats and intimidation.
➢ Racial, religious, gender or sexual slurs.
➢ Discrimination on the basis of age, gender, religion or culture.
➢ Harassment with repeated "hurry ups" etc.
➢ Manipulation of job specifications or withholding vital information to undermine work performance.
➢ Unrealistic workload or impossible tasks.
➢ Micromanagement.
➢ Changing work rosters to inconvenience particular employees.
➢ Assigning meaningless tasks unrelated to the job.
➢ Cyber bullying.
➢ Professional and personal exclusion or isolation.
➢ Career sabotage.

> ➢ Unjustified whistleblowing.
> ➢ Blackmail.
> ➢ Physical abuse or violence.
> ➢ Criminal assault.

Types of bullies

There are several typical types of bully, including:

(a) Ordinary workmates who are competitors wanting to impress the boss and weaken the position of those they bully. Often they are not very aware of their behaviour and will be repentant when it is pointed out.

(b) A manager or trade union official, often those new in the role who may lack confidence and/or competence and feel under pressure to prove themselves.

Managers who bully will tend to create a poor role model for others and be more likely to turn a blind eye to others that bully.

(c) People with type A personalities who are ambitious, driven, assertive and hostile.

(d) The psychopathic serial bully who bullies instinctively and may have an anti-social personality disorder. 1% of the population is psychopaths, the pathology of their condition including aggression, threats, lying and cheating.

Typical targets

Victims of bullying may:
> ➢ Be new on the job.
> ➢ Look or be different in some way, perhaps racially.
> ➢ Lack social confidence and tend to be loners.
> ➢ Show vulnerability and avoid conflict.
> ➢ Be from a different social or ethnic background.
> ➢ Be an academic type or 'nerd'.
> ➢ Struggle with some tasks.
> ➢ Be smaller or weaker, or have a disability.
> ➢ Be much younger or much older than the bully.

The effects of bullying

The effects of bullying can range from anxiety disorders, stress and depression to loss of confidence and eventual loss of job or career, as shown in Table 4.1.

Table 4.1. Effects of workplace bullying.

Type of effect	Effect
Physical	Insomnia Eating or drinking to excess Heart problems Stress-related illness Suicidal thoughts
Work performance	Distraction and poor concentration Loss of motivation Difficulty with new tasks Accidents working overstressed
Emotional	Fear and panic attacks Anger and frustration Depression Anxiety disorders Post-traumatic stress disorder
Financial	Loss of promotion Loss of second job Forced retirement Loss of income Loss of career
Social	Social difficulties Social isolation
Family life	Marital arguments over money etc. Separation/divorce

In short, bullying can ruin a person's life, leaving them unemployed for a long period, if not permanently.

For example, in moving to another University the first author was backstabbed with vicious rumours by his jealous previous boss and subsequently bullied also by a newly appointed boss. Eventually he resigned and, having had two mad and bad bosses in a row (and thus not having adequate referees) he never got another job.

Workplace bullying is also costly to industry because (Phillips, 2000; Burrell, 2001; Healey, 2011):

- Productivity and profitability are reduced.
- Motivation, teamwork and efficiency are reduced.
- Absenteeism increases.
- Expensive mistakes are made.
- An unsafe work environment results.
- Good employees leave.
- Time is wasted by bullying and in dealing with it.
- Unethical and fraudulent behaviours may occur.
- Adverse publicity circulates.
- There are costly compensation claims.

Dealing with bullying

Organizations can do a great deal to help reduce workplace bullying, for example by:

- Improving management training and skills.
- Running occasional workshops on proper workplace practices.
- Having a designated counselor to whom complaints about bullying may be addressed.
- Conducting surveys to determine the extent of bullying in the organization.
- When bullies are identified, any previous history of bullying in the current or previous jobs should be identified and investigated.
- Check the work performance of bullies.
- Refer bullies for psychological and/or psychiatric assessment.

The contact hypothesis

According to Forbes (1997): "The most frequently quoted statement of the (contact) hypothesis, provided more than forty years ago by Gordon Allport, says that prejudice may be reduced by equal-status contact between majority and minority groups with common goals, especially when this contact is sanctioned by law or custom (Allport, 1954, p. 281)."

This simple idea that bringing people who are in conflict (or when one is bullying the other) together will bring mutual understanding and reduce conflict often failed dramatically when first tried in multi-racial schools in the USA.

In fact, to reduce conflict other conditions are required, including:

(1) Remove conflict, as well as tackling the factors that lead to it.

(2) Equal status so that neither party has advantages over the other.

(3) Positive contact that is conducive to friendly and productive interactions.

(4) Typical contact: the representatives of each party must be typical members of it so that positive perceptions are generalized to the rest of the population.

(5) Social norms supporting inter-group contact.

(6) Common goals, including that of reaching a common understanding.

(7) Working as a team to improve the situation, neither party being able to terminate the process.

(8) No competition between groups.

Given such conditions, reduction of conflict at a more 'local' level (such as the workplace) is usually possible, at least for substantial periods of time. Reducing international and religious conflict, however, is a much more difficult task, as all history shows.

Proximity

People who live close together should tend to interact more frequently than those who live further apart, but they may not do so, and the difference between proximity and interaction is sometimes hard to differentiate.

A study in England found that white English people were more prejudiced against non-white immigrants who lived next door than those who lived further away (Schaefer, 1973).

An Italian study, however, found the opposite result. This showed a modest negative correlation between proximity and prejudice between 222 residents of Bologna against black immigrants living in the same neighbourhood (Kirchler & Zani, 1995).

It would appear, therefore, that in the English study the immigrants living next door were 'too close for comfort' and the occasional necessity for communication did more harm than good, perhaps involving cultural differences and language competency problems that made contact less than comfortable. With immigrants living only in the same neighbourhood, however, that gives an opportunity to get used to seeing them regularly without any requirement for communication.

From such studies Forbes (1997) concludes: "Contact in this sense seems to produce prejudice. But proximity to racial minorities or other immigrants at work seems to have the opposite effects: those with more contact show lower levels of racial and anti-immigrant prejudice."

This conclusion is in accord with some of the points listed in the preceding section, for example (2) and (7).

Mere exposure research

Persuasion studies on message repetition usually focus on the effects of repeated exposure to *information* about attitude objects. In a classic monograph Zajonc dealt merely with the objects themselves (Zajonc, 1968). Figure 4.1 illustrates the increase in attitude favourability with repeated exposure to three types of stimuli, showing a somewhat asymptotic behaviour similar to that of learning curves.

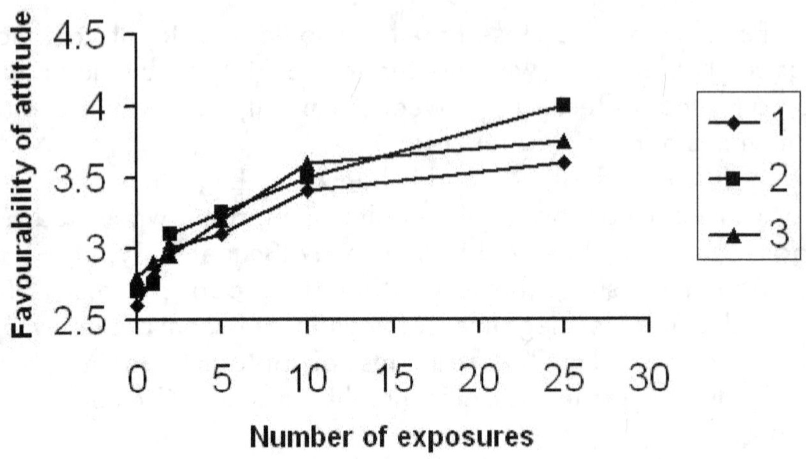

Figure 4.1. Increase in attitude favourability with increasing number of exposures to: 1. Turkish nonsense words. 2. Chinese-like characters. 3. Photographs of men.

This result is comparable to the 'set size effect', namely that increasing response is seen with increasing amounts of information, albeit repetition of the same information in the case of mere exposure.

It is also comparable, of course, to the learning curve of Figure 9.1.

One study found that the mere exposure effect reaches its maximum with 10-20 presentations, and others that longer series of exposures may eventually result in decreased liking. This latter result is comparable to the phenomenon of *advertising wearout* when excessive repetition of an advertisement has a negative effect.

Other studies of mere exposure, however, have yielded results more in line with the contact hypothesis. One found that college students repeatedly exposed to pictures of persons with different cultural backgrounds gave enhanced evaluations when their initial evaluation was positive, whereas they gave decreased evaluations when their initial evaluation was negative (Perlman & Oskamp, 1971).

This finding was also supported by a research finding that people who did not like abstract paintings on initial viewing showed increased dislike with frequent further exposure (Brickman et al., 1972).

Conclusions

Attitudinal psychology has, of course, obvious application to issues involving conflict, and Mohr's simple 'A+B+C+D' equation emphasizes that attitude changes with contact or information transfer.

The conditions for positive and productive contact suggested may prove helpful in resolving conflicts at a more 'local' level, for example relatively minor disputes and conflicts in schools, workplaces and suburbs.

As for the effect of proximity, there is no doubt that throughout history this has been a major factor in conflict, for example:

(1) Conflict between neighbouring tribes, just as has also been observed with chimps.

(2) Conflict between nearby city states as the first nation states evolved.

(3) Conflict between neighbouring countries as empires evolved.

(4) Conflict between empires and other regions as empires sought to expand.

Finally, mere exposure research does show that with increasing exposure to other people material we do become increasingly accustomed to them, even if we do regard them as friends.

Hopefully, some knowledge of attitudinal psychology, and the issues involved in workplace bullying discussed in preceding sections, will help readers cope with and reduce conflict in their lives.

4. Avoiding Conflict

Chapter 5

HEALTH

*I have had numerous discussions with physicians who acknowledge
that 10 percent calories from fat is the optimal level.*
Raymond Kurzweil, *The 10% Solution For A Healthy Life: How to
Eliminate Virtually All Risk of Heart Disease and Cancer* (1993).

*Women who are overweight when they are diagnosed
with breast cancer are twice as likely to die
of the disease as women who are of normal weight.*
Study published in *Journal of Clinical Oncology* (2004).

Introduction
To reduce aging, and decrease heart, stroke and cancer risk:
[1] Diet:
(a) Fruits, vegetables, fish and fibre wherever possible and
minimize fat, sugar, salt, caffeine and alcohol.
(b) Include foods that reduce cholesterol such as those rich in
omega-3 fatty acids, phytosterols and L-arginine.
(c) Include food rich in carotenoids such as beta-carotene and
lycopene, both of which are good antioxidants.
(d) Include food rich in antioxidant flavonoids such as grapes,
apples, cranberries, onions, broccoli, celery and tea.
(e) Have plenty of fluids to keep your blood reasonably thin.

[2] Diet supplementation:
(a) Cholesterol reduction: Lecithin and omega-3 fish oil & garlic
oil capsules.
Niacin, policosanol, or prescribed drugs on a temporary basis.
(b) Fat metabolism to assist cholesterol reduction: nicotinamide
(B3).
(c) For homocysteine folate, B6, B12.

(d) Antioxidants: selenium, vitamins A, C and E.
(e) Blood thinners: aspirin, a daily drink or two of red wine.
(f) BP, heart rhythm, variant angina: magnesium.
(g) General: multivitamin & mineral tablets.
(h) For skeletal health calcium.

[3] Exercise: to reduce weight, reduce triglycerides, increase HDL, strengthen the heart, replace fat with muscle, and elasticize blood vessels.

Calorie counting

The key to any weight loss and control program is a calorie counter booklet such as Alan Borushek's pocket-sized but invaluable *Calorie Counter* (Borushek, 2014).

With the aid of this little book you can quickly find out the calorie content of any food and drink that you have. Then you should write down what you ate and total your calories for a typical day. This can be compared to the number of calories appropriate for your ideal weight. Your ideal weight can be determined from the formulas

Men:

45 kg for 150 cm in height + 1.05 kg per cm taller   (5.1)
or   105 lb for first 5 ft in height + 6 lb per inch taller

Women:

43 kg for 150 cm in height + 0.9 kg per cm taller   (5.2)
or   100 lb for first 5 ft in height + 5 lb per inch taller

For example, a man of 183 cm in height should be 80 kg. This is at the top of the 5 - 8 kg range for a man with a 'medium' frame. For a small frame subtract about 5 kg, for a large frame add about 6 kg.

A woman 173 cm in height should be 64 kg. This is around the lower end of the 5 - 7 kg range for a woman with a 'medium' frame. For a small frame subtract about 4 kg and for a large frame add about 5 kg.

If you prefer Imperial units then a man 6 feet in height should be 177 pounds and a woman 5 feet 8 inches in height should be 140 pounds.

These formulae are approximate only and if they are too much for you refer to the charts in such books as Borushek's calorie counter (Borushek, 2014).

Now you must calculate the calorie intake appropriate for your ideal weight. You can do this using for following formula

Women: 1550 calories for 45 kg in weight + 20 cals/kg extra
or   6500 kJ for 45 kg in weight + 84 kJ/kg extra

For men add 500 calories.

This is for people in the age range 35 - 55. If you are older than this subtract about 300 calories and if you are younger than this (but more than 18) add about 300 calories.

For example, a woman of 45 who weighs 60 kg (for whom correct height according to Eqn 5.2 is 169 cm) requires

1550 + 15 X 20 = 1850 calories

A man of 45 who weighs 75 kg (for whom correct height according to Eqn 5.1 is 179 cm) requires

1550 + 500 + 30 X 20 = 2050 + 600 = 2650 calories

Note in passing a piece of trivia. We are supposed to have about six pints of blood. 2000 calories is enough to boil that amount of water about five times.

As the adjustments for age range might suggest, allowance should also be made for your level of activity.

If you are bedridden subtract from 500 to 900 calories depending upon your weight and a similar adjustment might be made for a crash diet (which I do not recommend at all).

If you are moderately active physically by way of your daily activities, for example in the skilled trades, add 250 to 450 calories depending upon your weight.

If you are highly active, for example a professional sports person, add from 500 to 900 calories depending upon your weight.

Well now, by way of the foregoing formulas, or from tables in countless books and magazines, you should be able to estimate your ideal weight and thence the appropriate calorie intake.

Body mass index

In losing weight the objective should be to get a couple of kilograms below the 'ideal weight' recommended by Equations 5.1 or 5.2, also aiming to make sure that your body mass index, that is:

$$BMI = (\text{weight in kg})/(\text{height in metres})^2$$

is somewhere around 20.

It may take months or even years to get BMI down to this conservative target figure but the objective is to eliminate excess body fat and a simple skinfold test[1] should be the final guide as to whether you have reached this goal.

The aim here is to help ensure, that along with appropriate diet and plenty of exercise, your body will burn up much of the cholesterol deposits that began to clog your blood vessels early in life.

The potential benefits are enormous:

[1] When you finally reach your 'fighting weight' you will, of course, be fighting fit, particularly as along the way you have become accustomed to a healthy diet and plenty of exercise.

[2] You will have reduced your statistical risk of vascular disease and cancer by around 50%.

[3] If you have already had symptoms of vascular disease, you should have been able to reduce these, if you started soon enough perhaps avoiding the need for major heart surgery later in life.

[4] A 1997 World Cancer Research Fund report concluded that 30 to 40% of cancers could be avoided with appropriate diet, regular exercise and not being overweight (Corder, 2007).

[5] If you are unlucky enough to be diagnosed with cancer then making your diet a little stricter and taking larger doses of antioxidant vitamins A, C, E and selenium might help you beat the disease, along with specialist treatment, of course.

---

[1] The skinfold test site for men is the waistline, for women either the buttocks or upper arms (Sudy, 1991). Special calipers can be used for accurate skinfold measurements (Marchese & Hill, 2005).

The 10% solution

Kurzweil (1993) advocates a 10% fat calories limit to *"virtually eliminate all risk of cancer and heart disease"* and backs this claim up with masses of WHO epidemiological evidence from around the world.

In contrast, recent studies using diets with 20% fat calories found little reduction in cancer and heart disease (*AMA J* 295 (2006) 629-4, 643-66).

The Ornish diet (1996) also advocates a 10% fat calories limit, and Christensen (2001) suggests that this "aggressive" limit is appropriate for a sedentary 60 year old man with CHD and a history of chest pain diagnosed as stable angina.

In a 5-year study an experimental group following the Ornish program of low-fat, whole-foods, vegetarian diet, aerobic exercise, and stress management training showed continued regression of arterial blockages and reduced LDL by 40% in one year, maintaining half this reduction at the end of five years. The control group, despite some of them receiving cholesterol-lowering drugs and some bypass surgery, deteriorated during the same period.

A further 3-year study of a control group of 139 and a group of 194 candidates for heart surgery following Ornish's program gave remarkable results.

The 194 heart surgery candidates all improved their blood lipid levels modestly (TC 202→183, LDL 123→102, HDL 37→42, TG 230→201), lost weight and 150 were able to avoid surgery during the 3 year program.

The 10% fat calories limit

Raymond Kurzweil's father died quite young of a sudden heart attack. Himself, finding the 30% fat calorie limit suggested by a doctor had not obtained the desired results, he decided to follow the Pritikin diet guideline of 10% fat calories. The results he obtained in 3 months are shown in the Table 5.1.

Table 5.1. Kurzweil's cholesterol lowering results, mg/dL.

	June 1987	October 1988	January 1989
% fat calories	40%	30%	10%
exercise calories per week	800	1,200	2,000
Total cholesterol	234	193	110
LDL		94	57
HDL	27	28	44
Triglycerides	616	354	43
TC/HDL	8.7	6.9	2.5
weight (lbs)	185	185	160
% heart risk	175	143	5

The results are impressive and it is the 10% fat calories limit, along with exercise and watching total calories in order to lose weight, that Kurzweil (1993) recommends as the key to reversing vascular disease and greatly reducing risk of heart attack, stroke and cancer.

Note, however, that at least 5% of calories should be fat to provide enough fat for the body, for example to maintain cell membranes and endothelium linings, and to provide energy for brain and other functions.

Comparing cholesterol reduction results

Table 5.2 summarizes the results obtained in four cholesterol reduction programs.

Briefly, these involved:

(1) 3 gm niacin daily, fat calories limit of 30%, moderate exercise, and oat-bran muffins had 2 or 3 times daily (Kowalski, 1987). Results are for 12 trial patients with good program compliance.

(2) 2.5 gm niacin daily, fat calories limit of 20% and moderate exercise (McGowan, 1998). Results are for one patient.

(3) 30% fat calories limit and 1200 exercise calories per week (Kurzweil, 1993).

(4) 10% fat calories limit and 2000 exercise calories per week (Kurzweil, 1993).

Programs (3) and (4) were consecutive and for Kurzweil himself.

Table 5.2. Cholesterol reduction results, mg/dL.

Program	1	2		3		4	
Duration	8 weeks	14 weeks		60 weeks		12 weeks	
Results	Change	Before	After	Before	After	Before	After
TC	-31.7%	251	155 (-38%)	234	193 (-18%)	193	110 (-43%)
LDL	-47.5%	172	84 (-51%)			94	57 (-39%)
HDL	+60.6%	41	48 (+17%)	27	28 (+4%)	28	44 (+57%)
TG	-42.1%	191	116 (-42%)	616	354 (-43%)	354	43 (-88%)

   The results clearly show:
(a) That high dosage niacin substantially improves cholesterol profiles (programs 1 and 2).
(b) That Kurzweil's "10% solution" does even better, whereas with a 30% fat limit results are poor except for a substantial triglyceride (TG) reduction. Notably, Kurzweil lost no weight in (3) but 25 pounds in (4) with a 10% fat calories limit.

   McGowan (1998) cites a further patient for whom high dose niacin improved cholesterol levels substantially. Furthermore, after a little over a year, blockage in the circumflex branch of his left coronary artery was reduced from 85% to 65%, a spectacular result that must have resulted more from 'relaxation' of the artery than from reduction in atheroma.

   As for diet, Borushek and Borushek (1981) claim that appropriate diet often reduces [total and LDL] cholesterol levels by 10 - 20% in 2 - 4 weeks, and by up to 25% in 6 - 8 weeks.

McGowan (1998), for example, cites the case of a patient with a TG reading above 2600 and HDL of 17 because of high sugar consumption. With simple diet changes, his levels were 298 and 24 only a month later.

Better still, Cooke and Zimmer (2002) note that a 10% fat calories limit can slow and even reverse coronary artery narrowing.

Most studies, of course, have single-mindedly involved one particular dietary supplement or restriction along with a little exercise.

Cooke and Zimmer (2002), for example, focus on high dosage L-arginine in conjunction with a so-called 'Mediterranean diet' which involves a much too liberal 34% of calories from fat.

The importance of exercise in improving lipid levels is exemplified well by a case study cited by Murray (1977) in which, after 4 sedentary days, 7 hyperlipidemic men were made to run 3 or 4 miles in 40 minutes on 4 successive days. Their triglyceride levels on days 4 - 8 were:

235, 173, 136, 119, 104,

an excellent example of how exercise rapidly reduces triglyceride and thence other blood lipid levels.

Epidemiological results

Kurzweil's book *The 10% Solution for a Healthy Life* (1993) used large amounts of World Health Organization data to establish by 'line of best fit to the data analysis' the following formulas for the risk of heart disease with increasing values of C = ratio of total cholesterol to HDL level:

Risk for men = 1.357 ln(C) - 1.1875

Risk for women = 2.069 ln(C) - 2.042

where ln( ) = natural logarithm. For example, a man with an acceptable total cholesterol level TC = 180 and a good HDL level = 60 has C = 3 and therefore risk = 0.30 or 30% of the average risk.

On the other hand a man with TC = 240, once deemed acceptable (just!), and HDL = 20 (levels almost this low are common) has C= 12 and thence risk = 2.18 or more than double the average risk.

Kurzweil's book also gives graphs of World Health Organization data for the incidence of three types of cancer in various countries of the world plotted against their average daily fat consumption F gm/day. Lines of best fit for cancer death rates per 100,000 people (R) were:

Breast cancer: R = 24(F - 30)/130
Colon cancer: R = 24(F - 30)/150
Prostate cancer: R = 16(F - 30)/130

Here F = 30 gives zero (in reality minimal) risk.
Then for F = 60 colon cancer risk is R = 24(60 - 30)/150 = 4.8
If fat consumption doubles to F = 120, then
$$R = 24(120 - 30)/150 = 14.4$$

and colon cancer risk has tripled.

This is because high-fat diets create a hospitable environment for anaerobic bacteria in the large intestine. Such bacteria can convert intestinal bile acids into carcinogenic acids. Apparently, weak acids like vitamin C inhibit this process.

To minimize cancer risk Kurzweil recommends limiting fat intake to 10% of total calories. Noting that 1 gm of fat produces 9 calories of energy 'zero risk' F = 30 gm gives 270 calories. If this is 10% of total calories then total calories will be 2700 calories, a reasonable amount for a moderately active young adult male (Borushek, 2014).

Kurzweil's findings are supported by the Australian National Health and Medical Research Council which says that 66 to 75 per cent of bowel cancer cases could be prevented by eating a healthy low fat, high fibre diet with plenty of vegetables and exercising regularly.

Note that excess sugar and protein in the diet will be stored as body fat if not used. Note also that the important role which glucose plays in cancer is emphasized by the success of new chemotherapy drugs that kill cancer cells by blocking their glucose metabolism.

Kurzweil goes on to point out that, although two out of three Japanese men smoke, the incidence of lung cancer in Japan is the lowest in the industrialized world and the incidence of heart disease is also very low because the Japanese diet is low in fat.

Kurweil's figures suggest part of the reason why the Moerman cancer therapy of low fat diet and high supplementation in vitamins A, C and E was found to cure vascular disease, namely that its very low fat intake reduces cholesterol levels (Jochems, 1990; Mohr, 2012c, 2013a, 2015, 2018a).

Conclusion

Maintaining a healthy body weight, regular exercise, plenty of relaxation, and a low fat diet will greatly improve general health and wellbeing, also considerably reducing risk of heart disease and stroke, cancer and diabetes.

If you do have concerns or symptoms of any kind, however, you should see your physician for advice.

As a beginning, have your cholesterol level checked. Total level can be checked in a few minutes at pharmacies but you should also have your LDL, HDL, Lp(a) and triglyceride levels checked too.

Ultra-low fat diets ($\leq$ 10% fat calories) should reduce all types of 'bad' cholesterol.

As the equations obtained by Kurzweil show, low fat consumption will also reduce cancer incidence, and the Australian National Health and Medical Research Council has said that 66 to 75 per cent of bowel cancer cases could be prevented by eating a healthy low fat, high fibre diet with plenty of vegetables and exercising regularly.

Chapter 6

A Positive Attitude

If I can conceive it and believe it, I can achieve it.
It's not my *aptitude* but my *attitude* that will determine my
altitude - *with a little intestinal fortitude!*
Jesse Louis Jackson, *Ebony,* August 1988.

The formative years

The period from age 12 to 30 has been termed the *critical period* for formation of attitudes and it can be divided into two parts (Morgan et al., 1979):

(a) <u>Adolescence</u>, during which parental, educational, peer group, advertising and sociological influences are largely responsible for development of most of the attitudes a person will develop through life.

(b) <u>Young adulthood</u>, a time when commitments such as choosing a vocation and marriage occur, and one in which attitudes tend to *crystallize* or 'freeze' for life.

In part this crystallization may involve attempts at *cognitive consistency* in which we tend to make our attitudes relatively consistent with one another and thus avoid *cognitive dissonance* or conflicting attitudes.

An example of this might be that a person who goes to considerable effort to maintain good health, for example by exercising regularly and maintaining a healthy diet, is less likely to smoke or condone doing so.

Heider's *balance theory* is of the cognitive consistency type and assumes that we try to maintain consistent and balanced or harmonious relationships with other people and our environment. According to this theory we would not marry a person with whom we disagreed on major issues about which we felt strongly, such as abortion (Morgan et al., 1979).

That attitudes do indeed crystallize or 'firm up' in young adulthood was confirmed by a US survey of women college students in the 1930s which, when followed-up 20 years later, found that for most issues on the 'conservative-liberal' dimension the women's attitudes, except for a slight "conservative drift" typical of older people, remained the same as they had been in their twenties (Newcomb, 1963).

That attitudes tend to firm up in adolescence and young adulthood has, of course, important implication for marketing along the lines of 'get-em young and get-em for life.'

Expectancy-value models of attitude and belief formation

The most popular models of attitude formation towards an object, action, or event, are the expectancy-value models of attitude formation which are expressed as a summation of evaluations of each of several attributes of the object of the form:

Attitude, $A = {}_{i=1}\Sigma^{n} e_i \, v_i$ (6.1)

where e_i is the *expectancy* about the object for attribute i, that is its score on a simple scale as to the subjective probability or extent to which the object has this attribute, v_i is the *value* or 'evaluation' of the attribute on a similar scale, and n is the number of attributes considered (Eagly & Chaiken, 1993).

For example, a person is reasonably sure that a new soft drink Choke a Dope has nice taste and is trendy but considers that it is too expensive. Using scales of 0 to 10 for e_i and -10 to 10 for v_i he might thus rate the soft drink as follows:

Attribute 1 (taste): $e_1 = 5/10$, $v_1 = 7/10$

Attribute 2 (trendy): $e_2 = 6/10$, $v_2 = 5/10$

Attribute 3 (price): $e_3 = 10/10$, $v_3 = -5/10$

giving an attitude score

$A = (5 \times 7 + 6 \times 5 + 10 \times -5)/100 = 15/100 = 0.15$

whereas a 'moderately good' score in which 5/10 is given for each expectancy and value would yield $A = 0.75$, whilst a 'middling' score of zero for each rating v_i would, of course, yield $A = 0$.

In practice there might, of course, be many more attributes and, perhaps, we might average the score as $A = {}_{i=1}\Sigma^n\, e_i\, v_i\, /n$, giving 0.05 in the foregoing example, and such scores have been found to correlate well with attitudes assessed by evaluative semantic differential items (Eagly & Chaiken, 1993).

Information integration models of attitude formation

The information integration theory of attitude formation calculates the response to a series of stimuli i as

$$R = w_0\, s_0 + {}_{i=1}\Sigma^n\, w_i\, s_i \tag{6.2}$$

where w_i and s_i are respectively the weight and scale of a person's attitude to a set of n items of information, and w_0 and s_0 are the weight and scale value of the person's initial attitude (Eagly & Chaiken, 1993).

Here the scale value of information is its location on the evaluative dimension and the weight is its *importance* or psychological impact in relation to the individual's judgment.

Simple summation models such as that of Equation 6.2 emphasize the importance of using multiple 'selling points' in advertising.

If the sum of the weights is required to be one then the model becomes an averaging model, but averaging models are more generally expressed as:

$$R = (w_0\, s_0 + {}_{i=1}\Sigma^n\, w_i\, s_i)/(w_0 + {}_{i=1}\Sigma^n\, w_i) \tag{6.3}$$

The initial attitude parameters w_0 and s_0 may in some instances, that of religion being perhaps the best example, represent 'intergenerational' attitudes acquired from a very early age from family and society at large.

Such initial attitudes, of course, may involve *prejudice*, for example ethnocentricity or racism, and, as history shows, such prejudices are often firmly rooted and perhaps could only be modeled by assigning them an exceptionally large weight.

More important in the modern consumer society, however, is social or imitative learning and in this context w_0 and s_0 represent initial attitude acquired by social learning from a peer or social group.

For example, a person believes that Christianity provides good moral codes (attribute 1) and that Christ did exist and provide a good exemplar of how we should live (attribute 2), but doubts that God really exists (attribute 3). Even if God did exist, however, in view of man's disastrous history he has a low evaluation of this last attribute, so that, using scales 0 to 10 for both w_i and s_i, he might thus rate Christianity as follows:

Attribute 0 (initial attitude): $w_0 = 5$, $s_0 = 5/10$ (i.e. 'halfway' values)

Attribute 1 (morality): $w_1 = 8/10$, $s_1 = 8/10$

Attribute 2 (good life model): $w_2 = 8/10$, $s_2 = 8/10$

Attribute 3 (God): $w_3 = 2/10$, $s_3 = 1/10$

giving a response score

$$R = [(5 \times 5 + 8 \times 8 + 8 \times 8 + 2 \times 1)/100]/[(5 + 8 + 8 + 2)/10]$$

$$= [155/100]/[25/10] = 1.55/2.3 = 0.674$$

whereas a 'middling evaluation score' with 5/10 for both the weights and scale values for attributes 0-3 would give $1/2 = 0.5$.

In contrast to simple summation models such as Equation 6.2, averaging models emphasize the need to have a limited number of effective selling points in advertising.

Measurement of attitudes

One of the earliest methods of psychophysical scaling was Thurston's *method of equal-appearing intervals.* In this a panel of judges rates each of a set of attributes of an object (for example a new product) according to an ascending scale such as 0 - 10. Then the mean value of the ratings of all judges is the scale value of the attribute on the attitude dimension. For example, Table 6.1 shows the scale values that might be established for a new soft drink Choke a Dope.

Table 6.1.
Example scale values for new soft drink Choke a Dope.

Attribute	Value on scale 0 - 10
I don't like it.	0
It makes me feel ill.	1
It is very sweet and must have lots of sugar.	2
It has a nice colour.	3
The bottle looks nice	4
My friends like it.	5
it is trendy.	6
The price is good.	7
It tastes nice.	8

Then for surveys, the mean of the scale values of the attributes selected by respondents is their assessment of an object. To obtain more reliable results attributes that are rated inconsistently by the judging panel are not used for surveys.

Likert's *method of summated ratings* was designed to be much easier to use than the method of equal-appearing intervals but to be at least as reliable. In this approach a large pool of items which are chosen intuitively for their relevance to the attitude object is used (Likert, 1961).

These items usually consist of statements of belief but statements about behaviours or affective reactions can also be used.

Typically each item is presented to respondents in a multiple-choice format such as:

1. Strongly disagree.
2. Disagree.
3. Undecided.
4. Agree.
5. Strongly agree.

Then, for example, a survey on attitudes towards women might contain questions like:

(a) Swearing is more objectionable from a woman.

(b) Intoxication in women is worse than in men.

With scores from 1 - 5 given to each of perhaps a dozen or so such questions the total score is then obtained for each respondent.

Desirably an initial pool of items should be pilot tested on a group of people to eliminate ambiguous and non-discriminating items which tend to result in neutral responses. This can be done by examining the *item-total score correlations*, each of which correlates the respondents' scores on an item with their scores summed over all the items. Then a good item will have a positive correlation and better items have higher correlations.

Likert Scaling is widely used in market research, for example to assess the response to political advertising campaigns.

Life assessment

One can assess the quality of a particular aspect of one's life using the Expectation-Value and Information Integration methods of attitude assessment.

To assess the quality of several key aspects of one's life the simplest and most widely used method is Likert Scaling.

Table 6.2 shows an example assessment for an adult person, scoring being done simply by using a printed copy of this table and circling the scores/ratings given to each of the items listed in the first column.

Table 6.2. Life quality questionnaire using Likert scaling.

Aspect of life: Circle the appropriate number	Very good	Good	Aver -age	Fair	Poor
Your work:					
1. Your job	5	4	3	2	1
2. Your pay	5	4	3	2	1
3. Relationship with boss	5	4	3	2	1
4. Workplace conditions	5	4	3	2	1
5. Relations with workmates	5	4	3	2	1
Your home life:	5	4	3	2	1
6. Your financial situation	5	4	3	2	1
7. Your home	5	4	3	2	1
8. Your parent(s) or partner	5	4	3	2	1
9. Your siblings or children	5	4	3	2	1
10. Your health	5	4	3	2	1
Recreation and social life:	5	4	3	2	1
11. Evening activities					
12. Weekend activities	5	4	3	2	1
13. Friends	5	4	3	2	1
14. Regular outings	5	4	3	2	1
15. Social, sport etc. groups	5	4	3	2	1
Your health:	5	4	3	2	1
16. General health	5	4	3	2	1
17. Fitness					
18. Diet	5	4	3	2	1
19. Weight					
20. Mental health	5	4	3	2	1
Add the numbers you circled:	**Score/100:**				

An 'average' rating of 3 on all 20 items gives, of course, a total score of 60. More important, perhaps, ratings of 1/poor for such important items as the first two (job and pay) might motivate one to try and improve these important life factors.

Similarly, a low rating for some of the health items might spur one into taking action to improve one's health.

In the wide range of items in Table 6.2 some items are much more important than others. Generally recreation and social life, for example, are not as important as one's job, and some jobs, of course, involve long hours 6 or 7 days a week, allowing little time for social life in any case.

Thus an evaluation such as that of Table 6.2 could be extended to include weights for each factor, as in the Information Integration method of attitude assessment discussed earlier, and this is done for the 'work' items of Table 6.2 in the following section.

Assessing a key aspect of life

One can assess the quality of a particular aspect of one's life using the Expectation-Value and Information Integration methods of attitude assessment discussed earlier.

As an example, we shall now assess the five 'work' items of Table 6.2 for a 'typical' person using the Information Integration method, giving the following result with weights and scores 1-10.

Attribute 1 (job): $w_1 = 5$, $s_1 = 5/10$ (i.e. 'halfway' values)

Attribute 2 (pay): $w_2 = 8/10$, $s_2 = 3/10$

Attribute 3 (relationship with boss): $w_3 = 7/10$, $s_3 = 4/10$

Attribute 4 (workplace conditions): $w_4 = 5/10$, $s_4 = 5/10$

Attribute 5 (relations with workmates): $w_5 = 4/10$, $s_5 = 5/10$

giving a total score

$$= 5 \times 5 + 8 \times 3 + 7 \times 4 + 5 \times 5 + 4 \times 5$$

$$= 25 + 24 + 28 + 25 + 20 = 122$$

whereas a 'middling evaluation score' with 5/10 for both the weights and scale values for all five items would give a total score of 125, so that the situation is perhaps 'satisfactory', for the present at least, but the low score of 3/10 for 'pay' is deserving of some attention sooner rather than later.

Conclusion

Having a positive attitude, along with self-confidence and hope, is a major key to success and happiness in life.

It is important, however, to assess one's life, and key aspects of it, in order to set goals and develop plans to improve those aspects of life, and thence one's life in general.

Table 6.1 shows how one can make a quick assessment of the quality of one's life using simple Likert scaling.

The following section then uses the Information Integration method to assess a 'typical' person's job, Table 6.2 then suggesting actions to take on the five key factors of this important life issue. Then, of course, the same approach can be used to examine other aspects of one's life, and decide upon actions to improve those aspects, including a timeframe for those actions.

As for quality of home life, in an article in Melbourne's Herald-Sun newspaper on 28/8/17 it was reported that a group of six "oldies" said that they thought such basic things as a sound diet, plenty of exercise, quality relaxation time, and a good social life to be the key to better health and happiness in old age. Their view illustrates the sort of simple, optimistic view of life that is likely to make life happier and more successful.

PART 2
LIFELONG LEARNING

Chapter 7

CONTINUING EDUCATION

When a man's education is finished, he is finished.
E. A. Filene, Attrib.

Introduction

Throughout one's career it is likely that some form of further learning will be required. Such *continuing education* may be obtained in a variety of ways:

[1] Courses, often short, at private colleges.
[2] TAFE courses.
[3] Postgraduate University courses.
[4] Continuing education courses run by Universities.
[5] Conferences and seminars run by professional associations.
[6] Meetings of special interest groups.
[7] Employer-run training courses.
[8] Courses run by community or government organizations.
[9] Self-education using magazines and books.
[10] Training packages available from companies such as Microsoft and Novell.

These options are briefly discussed in the following chapter.

Private colleges

Private colleges, most of them dedicated to a single area, offer full-time and part-time courses in such areas as:

- ➤ Aged care
- ➤ Art & design
- ➤ 0Audio engineering
- ➤ Beauty
- ➤ Business
- ➤ Child care
- ➤ Creative arts
- ➤ CIT, computer graphics/programming
- ➤ Counseling
- ➤ Fashion
- ➤ Horticulture
- ➤ Interior decorating
- ➤ Journalism
- ➤ Business/hospitality/tourism management
- ➤ Modeling
- ➤ Music performance & production
- ➤ Naturopathy
- ➤ Photography
- ➤ Reception
- ➤ Secretarial
- ➤ Travel & tourism
- ➤ TV production

Most of these offerings are of relatively short duration and are available part-time or by distance modes.

It is desirable that such courses are generally not more than 6 months full-time study to provide a clearly distinct option from that of TAFE and University certificate, diploma and degree courses.

With further study, in a few of these areas certificates at up to three levels are available and sometimes diplomas, advanced diplomas and degrees are also available, the latter sometimes in conjunction with a University.

TAFE courses

TAFE colleges also provide a comprehensive range of vocational short courses, for example:

➢ Business: import/export, project management, small business etc.
➢ Computing: databases, spreadsheets and word processing.
➢ Counseling: introduction, personal development, psychology etc.
➢ Drafting: autocad introduction & levels I and II
➢ Home renovation: masonry, owner building, timber framing etc.
➢ Furniture making: French polishing, upholstery, woodworking etc.
➢ Health: aromatherapy, massage, nutrition, reflexology etc.
➢ Horticulture: introduction, irrigation, landscaping etc.
➢ Hospitality: bar attendant, coffee making, food safety etc.
➢ Marketing: strategic selling, public relations
➢ Office skills: accounts, payroll, reception
➢ Trade skills: bricklaying, plasterboard, tiling, welding etc.
➢ Trade business skills: costing/estimating, site management etc.

In addition, many non-vocational courses are available, for example in acting, art, car maintenance, first aid, jewelry, languages, music, photography, recreation, weaving, and writing. Some of these courses do have vocational relevance.

Many TAFE courses are part-time ones for apprentices. Unfortunately, many apprenticeships are unreasonably long and bordering on exploitation of a cheap labour source. An example are hairdressing apprenticeships which take up to 6 years in Australia, certainly too long when most us would think a couple of weeks training would suffice.

Another looming problem is the slow introduction of diploma and degree courses in business to TAFE institutes when absurd numbers of people already do these in the Universities. Even MBA courses, let alone undergraduate business courses, are lightweight material that could and should be taught at school.

Postgraduate University courses

Postgraduate certificate, diploma and degree courses vary greatly between Universities and usually involve some 'tack on' or ancillary subject that sometimes could be made a specialist work area by graduates of appropriate degree courses.

Examples include graduate certificates and diplomas in:

➢ Accounting
➢ Architecture
➢ Building management
➢ Business
➢ Commercial law
➢ Computing
➢ Defence studies
➢ Disability studies
➢ Distance education
➢ Employment services
➢ Environmental engineering
➢ Human nutrition
➢ Human resource management
➢ Local government
➢ Management
➢ Management information systems
➢ Media studies
➢ Nursing
➢ Professional writing
➢ Psychology
➢ Software development
➢ Taxation
➢ TESOL (Teaching English for speakers of other languages)

These courses may be of interest and benefit to those already employed but in many cases it is doubtful whether they will improve one's employment prospects.

Students might be better advised to study the appropriate subjects in their first (and then perhaps only) degree studies. Later on a subject list could then highlight relevant subjects studied when applying for jobs.

There has been excessive proliferation in new University courses. My father used to joke about there being degrees in bee keeping in the USA. At the more reputable Universities there this may not be the case, but in Australia this has come to pass with degrees where none were needed before, examples being journalism, marketing, nursing and viticulture.

There has also been a plethora of new postgraduate certificates and diplomas and Masters Degrees. Some of these, such as courses in Sexology, Puppetry or Citizenship studies are either lightweight, absurd, or both.

The ubiquitous MBA deserves special mention. MBAs having been given out in literally absurd numbers, however, it might be best to be able to mention specific management experience and accomplishments on your CV in looking for promotion or a new job.

Alternately, one can buy an 'MBA in a book', and the first author published the *Scientific MBA* course he developed in the 1990s recently with Balboa Press (Mohr, 2017).

Continuing education courses

Universities occasionally run short 'continuing education' courses that generally run for a few days. These take on a single topic in a subject area but usually involve some 'recency' and thus may be a much quicker way of adding to one's knowledge later in life.

Other organizations, for example professional societies, may also run such courses from time to time.

Some courses run by TAFE and private providers may also involve relatively new or 'fad' topics such as naturopathy.

Conferences and seminars

Universities, professional societies, trade and other organizations occasionally run conferences and seminars that provide a forum for dissemination of new work.

These are therefore a useful way of acquiring new knowledge without taking much time to do it.

Special interest groups

Special interest groups, for example those for writers and artists, have regular meetings, workshops and other activities that may be helpful to their members.

Employer run training

Employers often conduct training, for example:

➢ Induction courses
➢ New equipment training
➢ Redeployment training

Employers may also 'outsource' training by arranging for other organizations to conduct training programs for their employees. They may also encourage attendance at TAFE and other short courses.

Community and government organizations

Sometimes local and state government, charitable and other organizations run information, counseling and training courses for the public.

These include such areas as drugs & alcohol, infant health and HIV or AIDS treatment.

In Australia Centrelink, the federal unemployment organization, runs and out sources courses in job seeking skills.

Conclusion

As an alternative to formal University, TAFE or private college courses there are now many courses available for study via the Internet, and home-based study is discussed in the following chapter.

Chapter 8

HOME-BASED LEARNING

There are some things which cannot be learned quickly, and time,
which is all we have, must be paid heavily for their acquiring.
They are the very simplest things and because it takes a man's life
to know them the little new that each man gets from life
is very costly and the only heritage he has to leave.
Ernest Hemingway, *Death in the Afternoon*, ch. 16 (1932).

Home schooling

In the USA home schooling has increased markedly in recent decades. The number of home-schooled children grew from just a few thousand in the early 1970s to 1.1 million in 2003, having increased 30% between 1999 and 2003.

In 2000, only 52 percent of colleges had formal admission policies for home-schooled students, but by 2005 85% did, in that year a study showing that home-schooled students scored 81 points higher than the national average on the SAT (Penn, 2007).

Though home-schooled children were only 2% of school-age children, they were 12% of the students in the National Spelling Bee and in three out of seven years a home-schooled child won the National Geography Bee (Penn, 2007).

In 2001, a home-schooled boy from Montana completed high school at 15. Not feeling ready for college, he wrote the novel *Eragon* which become a best-seller and was released as a movie in 2006 (Penn, 2007).

Certainly, therefore, children taught well at both home and school should do better!

Continuing education at home

In Chapter 10 'Real IQ' is discussed, proposing that continued learning in later life does increase intelligence.

This alone is considerable motivation for home-base learning for adults and in addition, of course, the acquisition of new knowledge and skills may improve one's career prospects.

In the context of 'making your children smarter', chapter 21 details of an experiment with rats that found that enriching their environment increased their brain size are given.

This provides further motivation for home-based learning in a comfortable, secure, cozy environment working at one's own pace, and at a time of one's own choosing, rather than sitting through uncomfortable classes being lectured by people often working straight out of some well-known textbook.

Informal self-education can occur through magazines and books, of course, and this is an important part of continuing education.

In general, however, self-education involves a 'credibility problem' so that it may be impossible to impress an employer with claims of some self-acquired knowledge or skill unless there is a good opportunity to demonstrate it.

Books on Human Resource Management, however, often point out that the best way of assessing the ability of a person to do a job is by actual observation of job performance

If a way can be found, therefore, to demonstrate the skills acquired when applying for a job or promotion it may help a good deal, demonstration of the product being a normal procedure for such things as advertising campaign proposals, architectural designs and product designs.

Distance education

We have long had correspondence schools and now 'distance education' using the Internet is the modern equivalent. In either case education is essentially by dissemination of information sourced from print media.

This begs the question one of the first author's fellow students at University who didn't think it was worth turning up to classes once asked him: *"Why don't they just give us the text books so we only have to turn up for the exams?"*

This was a very good question, and indeed this does now happen. In Australia, for example, several Universities now offer a wide range of courses over the Internet, with some exams conducted on campus.

Some of the more 'traditional' university courses such as medicine and engineering, however, are usually still run only on-campus.

On their website Open Universities Australia, for example, in 2018 were offering 194 degrees with 1409 subjects online to circa 370,000 students.

Courses offered included, for example only:

➢ Bachelor of Education (Early Childhood), Curtin University.
➢ Bachelor of Education (Primary), Curtin University.
➢ Bachelor of Applied Science (Construction Management), Curtin University.
➢ Bachelor of Commerce (Finance), Curtin University.
➢ Bachelor of Psychological Services, Swinburne University.
➢ Bachelor of Business, Swinburne University.
➢ Bachelor of Business, Griffith University.
➢ Bachelor of Criminality and Criminal Justice, Griffith University.
➢ Bachelor of Accounting, University of South Australia.
➢ Bachelor of Information Technology, RMIT (Melbourne).
➢ Bachelor of Arts, Macquarie University.

Australian Catholic University, ANU, Charles Darwin University, LaTrobe University, Murdoch University, University of New England also offer courses via Open Universities Australia, whilst Melbourne University, for example, offers a wide range of postgraduate courses online.

Overseas Universities also offer Internet courses, some requiring attendance at the University for a short period to complete the course.

There are also many private companies that offer Internet courses, usually a few months in length, and often with the exams taken online as well.

An early example of this was Microsoft and other software companies which provided manuals and software for self-learning of computer languages and system administration, with exams being taken to achieve certification as:

➢ Systems engineers
➢ Solution developers
➢ Product specialists
➢ Certified trainers

Conclusions

To excel in life you will always keep learning, essentially by self-learning whether that be by reading from a blackboard, PC screen or a book. In such ways education continues throughout

Short courses at private colleges are one option, but these are usually 'basic vocational' rather than 'additional career knowledge.'

A very convenient and economical alternative is such books as *The Scientific MBA* (Mohr, 2017), the section on Input-Output Analysis in Chapter 25 being an example of the very useful content of this book.

For starting a new business TAFE courses may help and the government's New Enterprise Incentive Scheme (NEIS) also offers help in building a business plan and subsistence payment for the first year of work in the new business.

Whatever your career, short courses, conferences, seminars and self-study can also play an important part.

Chapter 9

Effective Study Habits

Study more and criticize less.
This is a correct attitude towards learning.
Deng To, *Evening Talks at Yenshan* (1961-62),
quoted in *Literature of the People's Republic of China* (1980).

Skill learning

Learning some skills requires a large number of repetitions n, for example 'touch' typing where when fully proficient we do not have to consciously think of which key to associate with each letter of the alphabet to be typed. Such memory is called *procedural memory* or implicit memory.

Skill learning has three stages:

[1] The cognitive stage in which the requirements and components of the skill are learnt.

[2] The association stage in which the components are performed together and the skill is perfected.

[3] The automation stage at which the skill is completely remembered.

In learning skills *feedback* is important in stage [1] to help perfect each component of the skill and again important in stages [2] and [3] to help assess which components require further learning.

If the requirements of a new skill overlap those of one previously learnt *positive transfer* makes the new skill easier to learn. Conversely, if some parts of the new skill contradict those of an 'old' skill then *negative transfer* may make learning the new skill more difficult.

An example might be riding a bike where turning the handlebars to the right steers to the right. Used to this, in yachting one might have some difficulty becoming accustomed to pushing the tiller to the right to steer left.

Effective study

As prelude to thinking study may be needed and effective study techniques are desirable. In studying a chapter of a book, for example:

Motivate yourself and make time for the learning task. Relax for a while before starting to clear your mind, then summon your concentration and start, making sure there are no distractions.

Then apply the **HEART** routine suggested by Mohr (2014b, 2018d):

H. Skim through to see the different topics/sections in the chapter, trying to spot the highlight or key point in each.

E. Exposition. Carefully read through, not word for word, but focusing on the key points and searching for their meaning, if not already clear, in the surrounding text.

A. Again. Go through the material again, writing brief notes on the topics you identified in **H** with key words as headings, followed by brief elaboration of the key points.

R. Review the material to see how well you remember it, especially the key points.

T. Test how well you remember the material.

In studying *positive transfer* occurs when subjects overlap and well designed curricula take advantage of this wherever possible. When studying try to make a habit of letting previous learning help by noticing where subjects overlap in some way.

When we have negative attitudes towards a subject, however, *negative transfer* may occur. Hence the importance of motivating yourself for study, for example by thinking about the usefulness of the material under study.

Repetition and learning

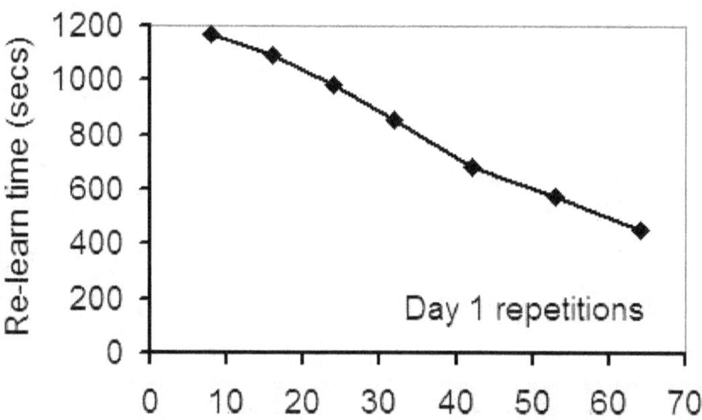

Figure 9.1. Influence of number learning repetitions on retention 24 hours later.

In a classical experiment Hermann Ebbinghaus found that after reading through a list of 16 syllables for 0, 8, 16, 24, 32, 42, 53, or 64 repetitions, and then 24 hours later assessing how many further repetitions were needed to re-learn the list, the result was the almost linear relationship shown in Figure 9.1.

This result shows that more practice (on day 1 here) gives greater learning. More important, it shows that each learning trial on day 1, which takes about 7 seconds, saves about 12 seconds on day 2. Thus it is better to spread learning trials out over time and this phenomenon is known as *distribution of practice* (Baddeley, 1990).

One trial of distributed learning had four groups learning to type with (Baddeley, 1990):

1. One session of one hour/day.
2. Two sessions of one hour/day.
3. One two-hour session/day.
4. Two two-hour sessions/day.

It was found that the first group learnt the keyboard more efficiently than the other groups. That is, the rate of learning per hour of practice was greater for the group with greater distribution of learning.

Learning curves

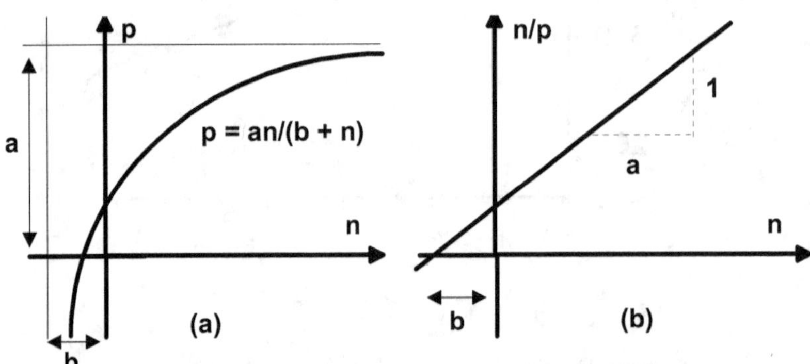

Figure 9.2. Mohr Plot for learning.

Suppose the degree to which a person or group has learnt something or been conditioned is given by the probability $p = 0$ to 1, and this probability depends on n, the number of repetitions of the learning process.

If we assume that the learning process is hyperbolic so that the degree of learning gradually increases towards 100% or the asymptote $p = a$ with $a = 1$, then this is represented by the hyperbola of Figure 9.2(a), the equation for which is

$$p = an/(b + n)$$

This equation is easily rearranged to give $n/p = (b + n)/a$ so that if we plot n/p against n the straight line of Figure 9.2(b) is obtained and the magnitude of the intercept with the n axis = $-b$ whilst, of more interest, the inverse slope of the line equals the horizontal asymptote a of the hyperbola.

In experimental situations this plot is useful in testing whether results are indeed hyperbolic and, if so, estimating the 'ceiling' value towards which some dependent variable is converging.

Applied to the memory of a single person, for example, a typical result might be $b = 3$, $n = 3$, giving $p/a = 50\%$, or 50% memory retention after three repetitions.

Here p is either:

(a) How well an item is learnt and people's names might be a good example of this, and generally we need about three repetitions of such things to remember them.

(b) How much of a 'block' of information is learnt. An example might be a list of names where, because of *interference,* words at the beginning (the *primacy effect)* and end (the *recency effect)* are remembered best.

For a slower learner, on the other hand, b might double to 6 so we need $n = 6$ to get $p = 50\%$ learning.

Applied to conditioning of the populace by advertising, p is the proportion of the population affected, and larger values of the asymptote b which flatten the curve might occur when there are two or more competing advertisers in the market. In politics this highlights the advantage of dictatorship.

In education it perhaps highlights the importance of avoiding conflicting messages so that it is often best to learn one subject at a time.

Forgetting

Figure 9.3 shows an example of *proactive interference* in which the accuracy with which lists are remembered declines as the number of lists learnt previously increases (Morgan et al., 1979).

Here the increasing number of previously learnt lists interferes with the learning of the last list. At the same time *retroactive interference* will occur so that learning of further lists reduces recall of the earlier lists.

A similar effect, called the *serial position effect,* applies to the items of a single list so that items early in the list are remembered better than those in the middle (the *primacy effect)* whilst items late in the list are remembered much better than those in the middle (the *recency effect).*

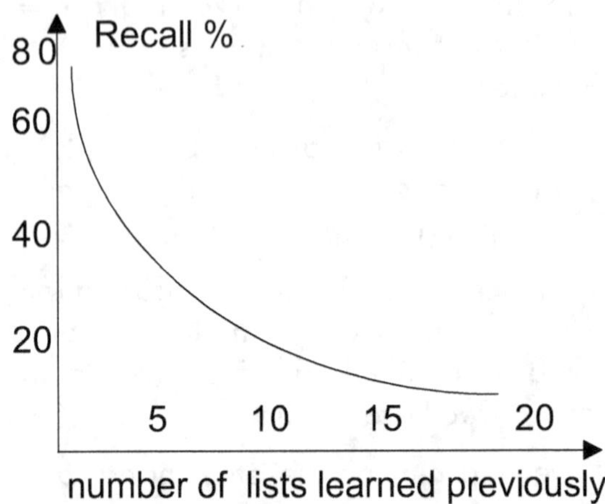

Figure 9.3. Decrease in recall of a list with increasing number of lists learnt previously.

Interference is one of the major causes of forgetting and forgetting curves generally take roughly the same form as that of Figure 9.3 where the curve is hyperbolic like that of Figure 9.2 but 'upside down.'

Interference is *trace-dependent* forgetting because of physical changes in memory traces when something new is learned.

Memory traces can also be changed by *decay* or by *motivated forgetting*, for example when we deliberately *repress* a memory.

Retrieval failure is when we lack or fail to use the right cues to retrieve stored memories. This is called *cue-dependent* forgetting.

Pseudoforgetting is when we fail to recall something, not realizing that it was not stored in LTM in the first place.

Generally, memory can decline with age, for example with the onset of senile dementia of the Alzheimer type (SDAT), Alzheimer's disease, or brain damage caused by injury, alcohol or other drugs.

Improving memory

Sometimes *mnemonic* techniques are used to improve memory.

The *method of loci* associates items to be remembered with physical objects in one's environment.

The *word peg method* typically uses a list of ten number-word pairs, for example one-sun, two-shoe and so on. Then to remember a list of food items the first two of which are bread and butter one might visualize:

[1] White bread as being bright like the sun,

[2] Our shoes slipping on butter on the floor.

The method may only be useful for one or two very important lists and can fix many items of a short list for many years.

An example of the *link method* is *narrative chaining* in which a list of words is remembered by inventing a story involving each item in the list.

The *method of word associations* uses a phrase with the first letter of each word corresponding to each item of a list, for example:

My very energetic mother just sits up near pop is used to remember the names of the planets in order from the sun, that is Mercury, Venus, Earth, Mars, Jupiter, Saturn, Uranus, Neptune, Pluto.

This method is often used by medical students to remember anatomical names.

Acronyms are another useful mnemonic in which words are formed from the first letters of a group of words, for example WHO for World Health Organization. Abbreviations of the names of companies (e.g., IBM) and mathematical and other methods (e.g., MIS = Management Information Systems) are also formed in this way.

The way in which text is remembered provides an insight into why key words are important in the memory process. It is believed that text is not stored in memory literally, but as a number of *propositions*, each of which has a *relational term* for which there are *arguments* (using the latter word in the same way it is used in connection with mathematical functions, especially when they are used in computer programs).

The sentence "Tom hit Jack", for example, is remembered as: (HIT, TOM, JACK)

If later "Tom apologized for hitting Jack" this is stored as

((APOLOGIZE, TOM), (HIT, TOM, JACK))

with the simple proposition of the original memory embedded in a complex one. Here the 'strong' word HIT acts as a key word and it is linked directly to the word TOM in long-term memory.

Conclusion

Human memories are often laid down in a split second and remembered permanently yet others, especially most of those laboriously lectured to us at school, are quickly forgotten:

Education is what remains, if one has forgotten
everything one learned in school.
Albert Einstein, *Out of My Later Years* (1950).

An understanding of memory processes can be some help in rectifying the situation, in turn contributing to better thinking.

In learning it is helpful to realize that interference occurs and that is often best to learn one 'block' of information at a time and then take a break to allow it to consolidate in long-term memory.

Figure 9.2 reminds us that deliberate learning requires some repetition, whilst Figure 9.3 reminds us not to try to learn too much new material at once, but to spread learning efforts over time.

Finally, the preceding section notes that mnemonic techniques are often a helpful memory aid, being much used by medical students, for example, to learn anatomical terminology.

Chapter 10

REAL IQ

Genius is one percent inspiration and ninety-nine percent perspiration.
Thomas A. Edison,
newspaper interview quoted in *Golden Book,* April 1931.

I have no great intelligence, I have imagination.
John Argryis, said to the first author in 1998.

Intelligence quotient (IQ)

In France, asked by the French government to do so, Alfred Binet (1857-1911) and his colleague Theodore Simon developed the first IQ test using questions that tested a child's attention span, recall capability, and problem solving skills.

In 1916, Stanford University psychologist Lewis Terman "tweaked" the Binet-Simon test to create the Stanford-Binet Intelligence Scale. In this, IQ is defined as a person's mental age score on an 'intelligence test' divided by their chronological age, the resulting fraction being multiplied by 100 to obtain the IQ score (Craughwell, 2012).

In the 1930s American psychologist, David Wechsler, developed three IQ tests: the Weschler Intelligence Scale for Children (WISC), the Weschler Preschool and Primary Scale of Intelligence (WPPSI), and the Weschler Adult Intelligence Scale (WAIS). These test results are compared to the results of other test takers in the same age group, and follow a Normal distribution with a median score of 100, with two-thirds of population scores being between 85 and 115, circa 5 percent above 125, and 5 percent below 75.

Multiple IQ tests

Differential aptitude tests (DAT) for verbal, numerical and 'abstract/figural' IQ are preferable, the final IQ being an average of these. Figural tests might take the form of Raven's matrices which typically show 3 rows of 3 simple diagrams with the last diagram omitted, followed by several diagrams, one of which is the correct one to 'complete' the 3X3 matrix (Mackintosh, 2011).

Example IQ test

In each question a missing number is to be deduced according to some logical arithmetic operation or sequence. In these example questions the answers are the numbers following a question mark and underlined (Mohr et al., 2017). The test the time allowed for these 10 questions would be circa 8 - 10 minutes.

Find the missing numbers:

[1]   6   7   9   13   21   ?<u>37</u>

[2]   447   (386)   254
       262   (?<u>518</u>)   521

[3]   4   7   9   11   14   15   19   ?<u>19</u>

[4]   2   10   6
       3   9   3
       1   3   ?<u>1</u>

[5]

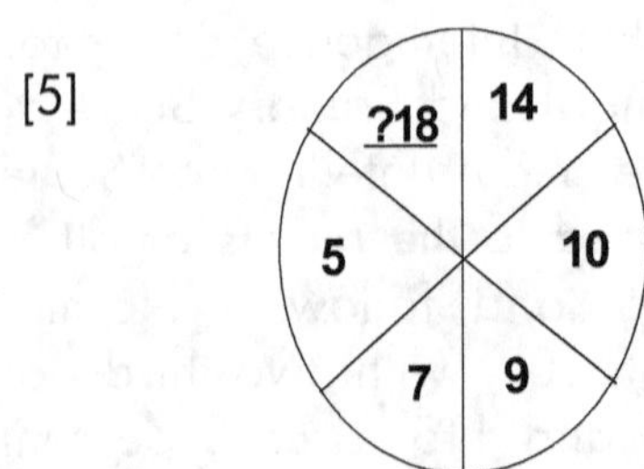

[6]   279   242   205   168   ?<u>131</u>

[7]   13   (78)   12
      11   (?<u>55</u>)   10

[8]   126   62   30   14   ?<u>6</u>

[9]   7   1   2
      5   4   1
      3   2   ?<u>5</u>

[10]

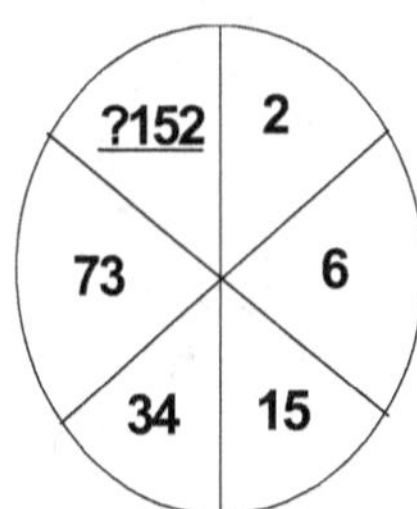

Keys to answers:
[1] The increments double.
[2] Middle number is twice the difference of the others.
[3] Alternate sequences (+3, +2, +1, +0) and (+2, +3, +4).
[4] 3rd # in row = 2nd - 2 x 1st.
[5] Diagonally opposite number is double.
[6] Decrements of -37.
[7] Middle number is half the product of the others.
[8] Next # = half x last # -1
[9] Sum of rows = 10
[10] Going around next # = 2 x last + 2 (then + 3, + 4 etc.).

If the scoring system for Craughwell's 10 item tests is used then 16.5 points are given for each correct answer, ratings for various scores then being (Craughwell, 2012):
165 Genius
148-132 Gifted/superior intelligence
115 Higher than usual intelligence
99 Average intelligence
83 Low average intelligence
70 or below, very low intelligence

For more on IQ tests, for example the SAT test, and 'types' of intelligence (e.g. "Gardner's Eight Intelligences") see *In Search of the Human Mind* (Sternberg, 1998).

How important to success is IQ?

Gladwell cites research that shows that IQ beyond an average of 120 "doesn't seem to translate into any measurable real-world advantage" (Gladwell, 2008).

According to Butler-Bowdon, "You just have to smart *enough*", and beyond this point it is "traits of personality and character" that make all the difference (Butler-Bowdon, 2017b).

British psychologist Liam Hudson said: "A mature scientist with an adult IQ of 130 is as likely to win a Nobel Prize as one whose IQ is 180" if he or she develops more systematic research skills, broader knowledge, and better networking to get ahead in the workplace.

Lewis Termann tracked children with high IQ into adulthood, finding that family background was a more important factor in real-life success than IQ, the most successful coming from homes "filled with books", half of them having a university degree at a time when these were much less common (Butler-Bowdon, 2017b).

Often the most important factor in achieving high levels of success is 'practice', the "ten-thousand hour rule" saying that to be very good at something requires at least 10,000 hours of deliberate practice (Gladwell, 2008).

An example, perhaps, were the Beatles who by the time they toured America in 1964, had performed on stage 1,200 times.

A little luck was also required, however, namely a chance meeting between their manager and a German impresario that led to their period of residency in Hamburg when they sometimes performed two or three times a day.

Thus Butler-Bowdon concludes: *Success is never down to a single thing, but it is rather a combination of talent, work, luck, and environment* (Butler-Bowdon, 2017b).

Real IQ

Intelligence is part inherited and part developed thereafter by learning and experience, often referred to as 'nature and nurture.' It is claimed that IQ tests are "a standardized examination devised to measure human intelligence as distinct from attainments" (Carter, 2007), but many argue that they largely measure learning, not innate intelligence.

It is generally assumed that IQ peaks at age 18, about when 'developmental' school education is finished in advanced countries. We contend that further education and study, however, should be able to increase IQ further so we propose a *real IQ* calculated for those over 18 as (Mohr et al., 2017):

Real IQ = IQ(18) − a(disease/injuries)

+ b(years of learning since 18)

+ c(creativity) - d[(age -18) if over 18]

Here IQ(18) is that one develops, all going OK, by age 18 as a result of hereditary factors and education and 'a', 'b', 'c' and 'd' are constants.

These constants have the following roles:

(a) 'a' is a constant to calculate reduction in IQ resulting from any disease or injuries acquired later which affect the brain, including Alzheimer's disease and psychiatric conditions such as depression.[2]

(b) 'b' is a constant, perhaps circa 0.25, for the effect of learning after the age of 18.

(c) 'c' is a constant for creativity, perhaps circa 1 − 2 if creativity is measured on a scale of 1 to 10.

(d) 'd' is a constant for normal decline in intelligence with aging, perhaps about half the value of the constant 'b'.

---

[2] In contrast to depression, note that positive attitudes may improve real intelligence, an example being the 'teacher expectancy effect.'

In the terms involving the factors 'b' and 'd' the notion of 'use it or lose it' is considered, that is, learning doing intelligent things should help further increase one's intelligence, just as doing more exercise should help strengthen one's muscles.

Creativity is obviously an important factor because if one has considerable ability, but no inclination to put it to tangible use, then one cannot be seen as having much real intelligence.

Whether creativity is, to any extent, in one's genes is debatable, but probably it is mostly a learnt trait, but one that relates to intelligence. In other words, without much ability to create, or intelligence, one is not likely to be very creative.

The foregoing simple equation should, indeed, encourage people to indulge in vicarious learning, surely the best kind for usually people are able to tackle subjects that genuinely interest them with more enthusiasm. In addition, being free to choose when and how one studies may improve results, of course, as this is far less painful than the all too many years spent listening to teachers regurgitate material from text books they have relatively little understanding of.

In our view, it also helps explain how people like Leonardo da Vinci and Isaac Newton, despite having only had very basic schooling, could achieve so much, namely because they did all the work themselves, whereas now most academics have research student slaves [effectively an apprenticeship historically (Mohr, 2013b; Mohr et al., 2018e)] to work on often silly topics they dream up.

Finally, an example of the great 'plasticity' of the brain was a US woman, Michelle Mack, who was found when well into her twenties to have been born with nearly all the left side of her brain missing. Nevertheless, her brain having 'rewired' itself, she had "fairly normal language abilities" and only relatively minor difficulty in coping with abstract concepts and visual-spatial processing.

Social and emotional intelligence

'Social intelligence' and 'emotional intelligence' are closely related, and tests of social intelligence include questions about how people would feel in certain social situations, and questions about the emotions shown in pictures of people smiling or frowning.

Some EI tests use self-report questionnaires, and according to Mackintosh (2011): - *a distinction needs to be drawn between self-report questionnaires, which seem to be a largely measures of well-established aspects of personality, and more objective measures which may more reasonably be called measures of intelligence.*

Performance on the Mayer-Salovey-Caruso Emotional Intelligence Test (MSCEIT), for example, improves with age, and females usually do better than males. Assessments of social behaviour by teachers, friends and managers, however, sometimes show negative correlations with EI test scores (Mackintosh, 2011).

Genetic factors

Genetic defects can, of course affect coefficient *a* of the foregoing formula for Real IQ, for example Fragile X and Down's syndromes, and degrees of mental retardation can fall into four classes:

> Mild.
> Moderate.
> Severe.
> Profound.

Then there are external influences such as malnutrition, lead poisoning and foetal alcohol syndrome, to name just a few. Depressive illnesses, even being slave to a lousy, bullying boss could also be a factor.

What is needed for best results, whether in the home, school or workplace, is an 'enriched environment' and positive attitudes and encouragement to obtain better results, and rewards at least occasionally when better results are obtained.

Finally, as noted in the recent book *Human Intelligence, Learning Behaviour* (Mohr et al, 2017), such substances as lecithin, magnesium fish oils, zinc, and vitamins A, B-group, C, D and E are helpful in improving brain function, especially in the very young and the very old (Holford & Colson, 2008).

Conclusions

It is generally assumed that IQ peaks at around the age of 18, that is, at about the time when we finish school.

It is important to realize, therefore, that 'real IQ' in fact should increase in later life, rather than decrease as generally assumed, if we continue learning and thus continuing to build both our knowledge and the neural networks in our brains.

It is also important to realize the 'real' or 'effective' intelligence requires creativity, so a factor for this is also included here in the calculation of Real IQ.

Chapter 11

THINKING AND PLANNING

*Faith is a charisma not granted to all; instead man has the gift
of thought, which can strive after the highest things.*
Carl Jung, *A Psychological Approach to the Dogma of the Trinity,*
(1958), *Collected Works,* vol. 2 (1969).

The tools we use for thinking

What we have learnt and can remember is basically what we have to think with. In other words, we can't think meaningfully about things we know nothing about.

Thinking uses four elements:

[1] Images.

We often use *visual imagery* in thinking. For example, we often find it easier to describe:

(a) The shape of something by sketching it.

(b) A physical operation by demonstrating it.

In connection with example (b) the term *muscular imagery* is sometimes used to describe the way in which we remember complex physical movements.

[2] Symbols.

Language involves the spoken and written use of symbols. These symbols can be words, mathematical formulae, pictures (including diagrams, maps and graphs) or gestures that represent either *objects, operations, relationships* and *qualities.*

Most obviously we use language to communicate with one another. Language also plays an important part in thinking, making it possible to perform mental processes such as analyzing, synthesizing, thinking abstractly and generalizing. For example, we usually have to 'collect our thoughts' in deciding what to say to someone and this is a thinking process.

[3] Concepts.

Concepts can be defined as categories that represent a class of objects, events or qualities wherein each item has a number of common features. A simple example is birds which 'mentally' are a concept and birds have common properties such as two legs, wings and the ability to fly and lay eggs.

Some birds, like the ostrich or emu that do not fly, do not fit this bird concept so well so that in the hierarchical structure of semantic memory we might store the concept of birds as a 'heading', associating with it the 'universal' features of two legs and feathers. Below this in the 'top-down' tree structure (i.e., really a root structure perhaps) may be storage locations for the two sub-categories of birds that fly and those that don't.

Such categorization is important for both efficient learning and memory storage, and efficient recall and thence thinking.

When driving, for example, when you see a set of traffic lights (a concept) you note which colour is 'on' and quickly decide (a thinking process) what action to take.

As noted, *natural concepts* like birds may involve atypical examples. More abstract concepts like 'bad' and 'nice' are even more 'fuzzy' and the criteria we each associate with such concepts vary considerably.

Learning of concepts is made easier by *transfer* when they are similar to already familiar concepts.

[4] Rules.

Rules involve connections between features of a concept and between different concepts.

In the case of traffic lights, for example, we should know the rules and have only to choose 'yes' or 'no' as to whether we follow the appropriate rule. Indeed, in a split second may be all we have time to do so.

The rule for traffic lights might be represented as

(green = go) OR (amber = slow down) OR (red = stop)

and the rule for driving might be written

(accelerator = go) OR (no accelerator = slow) OR (brake = stop)

so to stop at a red light we have to connect the two rules, a process probably carried out in short term memory.

Here a good exercise would be to write BASIC coding to combine the two foregoing rules in the same way our brain might handle it. In a 'traffic light' segment of code an INPUT statement could read in numbers 1,2,3 to corresponding to green etc., using these to direct execution appropriately to a 'driving' code segment in which the 'flags' 1,2,3 determine which message of GO etc. is printed to the screen.

Critical thinking

Many of the tools used for critical thinking, such as decision trees and tables, are usually prepared by one or two people for presentation to a group of people at a meeting.

'Decision theory' is a somewhat imprecise term sometimes used to refer to techniques for making business decisions. Critical thinking also refers to the process of examining one or more alternative ideas or proposals and deciding which, if any, to choose.

Critical thinking to determine the best of a number of alternative solutions to a problem typically involves such steps as:

[1] Define the problem and the criteria that a solution must meet.

[2] Compare alternative solutions to these criteria.

[3] Evaluate which solution best satisfies the criteria.

[4] Revue this decision.

Benefit-cost analysis, which is discussed later in the present chapter, is a good example of critical thinking based mainly on financial considerations.

Serendipity

This word was invented in the 18th century by the English man of letters Horace Walpole when inspired by the Persian fairy tale "The Three Princes of Serendip" whose heroes often made discoveries by chance.

In their book *The Art of Insight, How to have more AHA! moments,* Charles Kiefer and Malcolm Constable (2013) say:

> *Insights, wisdom, and good judgment come from a clearheaded, calm, and focused state of mind.*

Serendipitous ideas, however, are unpredictable. Sure, they may come after weeks, months, or even years of working on some problem. But they may come when awakening from a dream in an REM stage of sleep when the brain is 'reorganizing' itself, or at almost any other time of day when the some thought passes through the brain which is perhaps related to the problem in question.

There is no doubt, however, that those who have a habit of trying to come up with new ideas will have more serendipitous moments, and no doubt Edison's 1093 patents came about as a result of his having his own home laboratory in his teenage years (Heyn, 1976).

Perhaps one of the best examples of serendipity was the discovery of penicillin as a result of a lab door being left open accidentally, contaminating a Petri dish on the floor below.

Another was Henri Bequerel's discovery that fluorescent radium salts produced good photographic images on bad weather days without much light. Repeating his experiments in a dark room confirmed this result, and he gave the task of finding the source of the radiation and explaining it to Marie Curie as the topic of her doctoral thesis (Maccinis, 2009).

Decision matrices

An example is the 'prisoner dilemma matrix' where two prisoners are interrogated separately. What happens if neither, one or both confess?

Prisoner B	Prisoner A	
	Confess	**Don't**
Confess	Both - 20 years	A Life B 10 years
Don't	A 10 years B Life	Both - free

The table shows that the best option is clearly that neither should confess, giving a simple example of how it is usually best to seek advice on, and involve others in important decisions.

Decision tables

A good example is the following table of the performance of three categories of stocks and shares under boom, steady and slump market conditions.

	Boom (a)	Steady (b)	Slump (c)
Gilt edged (x)	5 %	5	5
Speculative (y)	20	0	-10
Unit trusts (z)	10	5	0

What then is the best mix of shares to buy?

The *deterministic solution* is as follows. For a 10 year cycle time in business conditions assume $a = 1$, $b = 6$ and $c = 3$. Then the profit (%) from each of the three share types is:

$$x: \ 5 + 30 + 15 = 50$$
$$y: \ 20 - 30 = -10$$
$$z: \ 10 + 30 = 40$$

so that one should buy x or z but not y (unless boom conditions are assured for a known period).

Mind maps

Mind mapping was created by Tony Buzan (Norcan, 1999) and is sometimes a useful way of getting ideas down on paper.

A mind map begins with map title (title branch) at the centre of a blank page, typically a project to be undertaken. To this thoughts are added as *child branches*. Typically these will be actions or tasks that need to be done to complete the project. Some, if not all, of these tasks will involve several smaller tasks and in this way a mind map grows out from the central title.

Advantages of mind maps are:

[1] That they can be written down quickly as only key words are used to describe each element of the map.

[2] They are easy to read and are ideal for presenting ideas on a board to an audience.

[3] They are a good way of getting an overview of a project or proposal.

[4] They lend themselves to 'evolution' as new ideas are added.

Mind maps can be used for:
- Group brainstorming sessions
- Presentations
- Decision-making
- Note-taking
- Planning
- Summarizing projects or proposals.

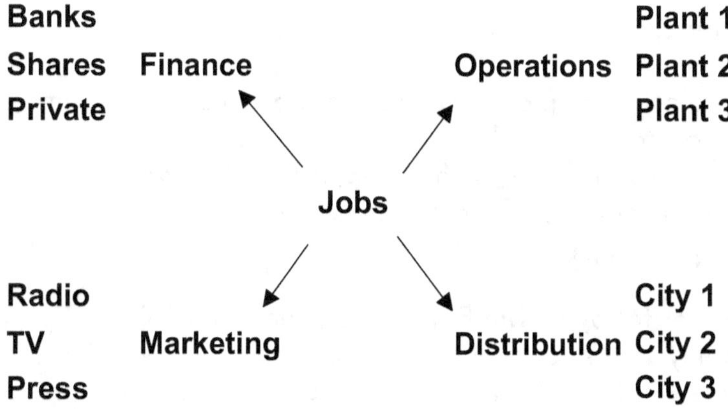

Figure 11.1. Mind map of company activities.

Figure 11.1 shows an example of a mind map for the CEO of a small manufacturing company. This reminds him of the four basic functions of finance, manufacturing, marketing and distribution.

These four items are then broken down further and additional information such as the names of the personnel responsible for each of the activities could easily be added to the map.

Probability trees

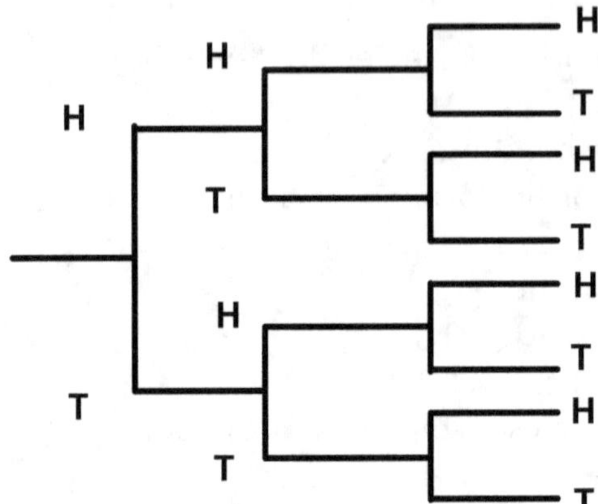

Figure 11.2. Example of a probability tree.

The simplest example is that of tossing a coin three times. All possible outcomes are shown in Figure 11.2.

This is a special case of the *binomial distribution* and, for example, the probability of three successive heads is

$$P(H/H/H) = (1/2)^3 = 1/8$$

and the answer follows from Figure 11.2 because $P(H) = P(T)$.

Probability trees are of little use but the idea can be incorporated with that of a decision tree to assist in important business decisions.

Decision trees

Decision trees are sometimes a useful way of depicting business strategies. A simple example is that of a manufacturer asked by a supermarket chain to make a 'home brand' version of its product, a decision tree for which is shown in Figure 11.3.

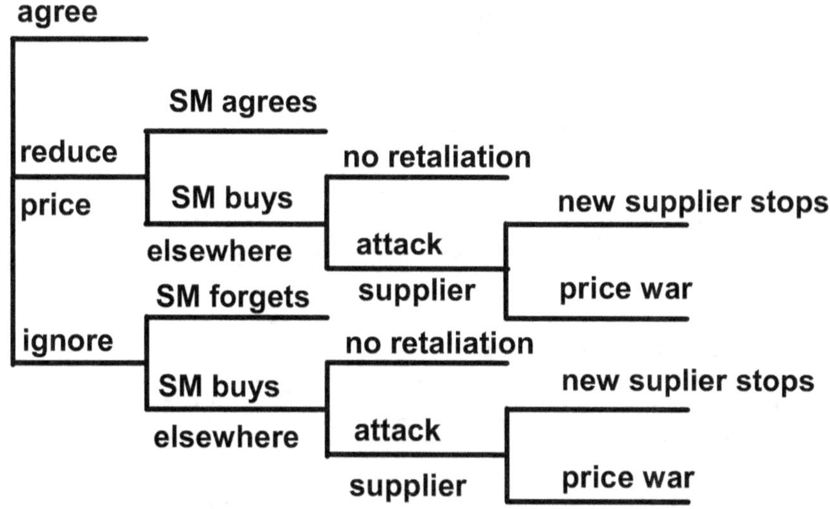

Figure 11.3. Example of a decision tree.

As another example Figure 11.4 considers the problem of deciding whether to launch a rocket at a certain time or not, attaching probabilities and profit figures to the decision tree.

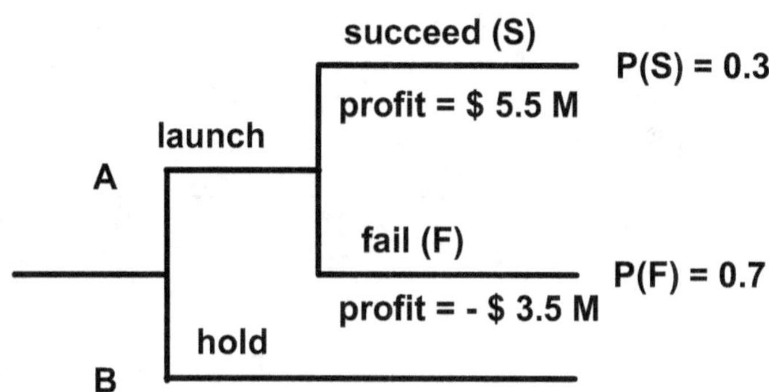

Figure 11.4. Decision tree with probabilities and financial outcomes.

Then the Expected Monetary Value (EMV) of a launch is 0.3(5.5) - 0.7(3.5) = - $0.8M so we should decide to hold.

With more optimistic figures, for example P(S) = 0.7 and P(F) = 0.3, the EMV of **A** is $2.85M and the launch decision is much more favourable, though perhaps still not certain.

Benefit-cost analysis

As an example of this widely used procedure consider the problem of developing a road repairs program for which the costs of the various levels of repairs or reconstruction are shown in Table 11.1.

Table 11.1. Cost of road operations.

Operation	$k /lane km
P Patching	10
T Topseal (25 mm)	20
S Reseal (50 mm)	50
F First two courses	100
R Reconstruction	200

Table 11.2 shows the various types of road works to be carried out and the years of service provided by the treatments of Table 11.1.

Table 11.2. Required works and longevity of the options.

Road type	Lane km to repair	Years of service P	T	S	F	R
A Residential	30	2	5	10	20	50
B Residential feeder	20	1.5	4	8	15	45
C Signaled arterial	10	1	3	5	10	30
D Freeway	5	0.5	2	3	5	10

Then the years of service in Table 11.2 (the benefit or return r) are divided by the corresponding costs c of Table 11.1 to give the *benefit-cost ratio* or r/c results of Table 11.3.

Table 11.3. r/c ratios for the various options.

Road	Operation				
type	P	T	S	F	R
A (30)	0.20	0.25	0.20	0.20	0.25
B (20)	0.15	0.20	0.16	0.15	0.225
C (10)	0.10	0.15	0.10	0.10	0.15
D (5)	0.05	0.10	0.06	0.05	0.05
c	(10)	(20)	(50)	(100)	(200)

The 'best' construction program is formed by giving priority to those activities with the greatest r/c ratios.

Then, choosing the larger r/c ratios in Table 11.3 the construction program is determined, as shown in Table 11.4.

Table 11.4. Works program selection.

Stage	Option	δC	δQ	C	Q
1	A/T	600	150	600	150
	A/R	6,000	1,500		
2	B/R	4,000	900		
	B/T	400	80	1,000	230
3	C/T	200	30	1,200	260
	C/R	2,000	300		
4	D/T	100	10	1,300	270
	D/S	250	15		

For the first step of the program the two largest r/c ratios (both 0.25) are considered, that is the A/T and A/R options (where A = row and T = column) in Table 11.3.

For these the increment in total cost or δC values are given by multiplying the figures in brackets for the appropriate rows and columns in Table 11.3. Then the increment in total benefit or δQ values are given by multiplying the 'km' and 'Years of service' values in Table 11.2.

Then the A/R option is rejected as too costly, so that stage 1 of the program is A/T.

Next we choose the B/R and B/T options, respectively with r/c = 0.225 and 0.20, finally selecting the second, the first being too costly.

Now, assuming we desire a spread of activity over all types of road (A - D), we next compare C/T and C/R, both with r/c = 0.15, choosing the cheaper option again for stage 3. Now requiring a D component for stage 4 we select D/T with the maximum r/c value for this road type.

Figure 11.5 shows the benefit-cost curve for the program selected in Table 11.4 and this takes the required form (that is, the slope diminishes gradually).

Such approaches may seem relatively tedious and mathematically trivial at first sight but in practice the data of Tables 11.1 and 11.3 is generally constant, the main variable being the quantities or work required in Table 11.2.

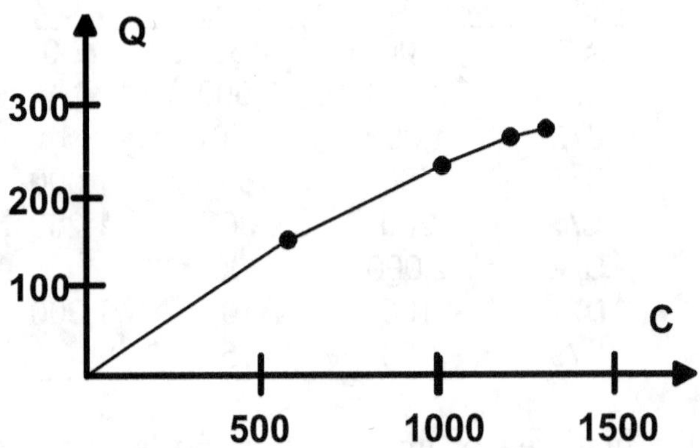

Figure 11.5. Benefit-cost curve for the program of Table 5.5.

Conclusion

Decision trees, especially if they have probabilities and costs attached, are useful tools in the decision making process.

Decision tables are also useful, especially if they have weighted quantities to enable a total score to be given to the alternatives under consideration.

Benefit-cost analysis has been included here as it is, essentially, a decision table method, albeit once involving a number of (consecutive) decisions or selections.

Finally, we should always remember that, as the 2010 book *Bozo Sapiens* seeks to remind us, "to err is human" (Kaplan & Kaplan, 2010). Nevertheless, critical thinking using such methods as those discussed in the foregoing chapter should help avoid making bad decisions.

Chapter 12

CORPORATE STRUCTURE AND PLANNING

Government of the busy by the bossy for the bully.
Arthur Seldon, *Capitalism* – subheading on over-government (1990).

Corporate structure

Corporate structure is the hierarchical structure and communication channels giving rise to the chain of command and response in a company or organization. Some of the basic types of corporate structure are:

[1] Functional structure. This is the usual structure for small companies and corresponds to one division of type (2) below.

[2] Divisional structure. For a corporation with just two divisions this is of the form of Figure 12.1.

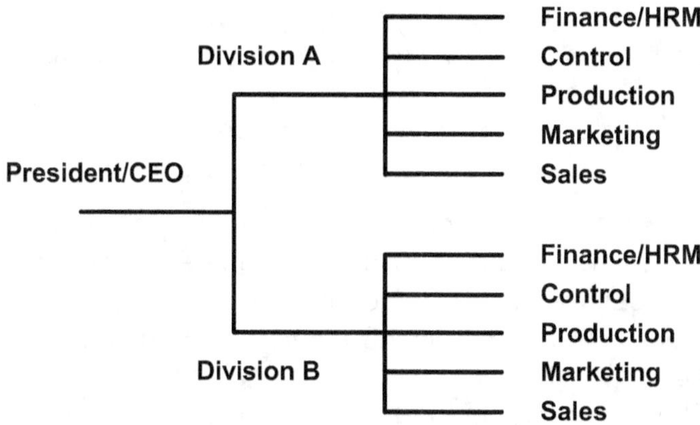

Figure 12.1. Divisional corporate structure.

[3] Matrix Structure

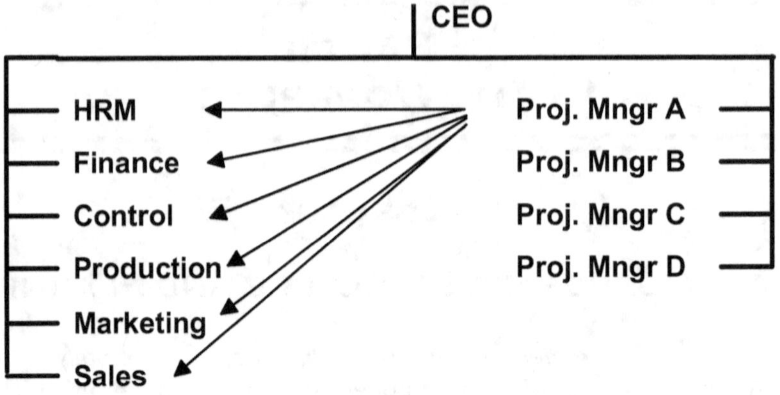

CEO

HRM   Proj. Mngr A
Finance   Proj. Mngr B
Control   Proj. Mngr C
Production   Proj. Mngr D
Marketing
Sales

Figure 12.2. Matrix organization structure.

Note that in Figure 12.1 Finance and HRM are combined into one group, but not in Figure 12.2. Similarly, marketing and sales might often be one group. In a very small business, of course, the boss or owner is HRM/control/marketing, finance is the bank a few doors away, and the few employees may be production and sales.

[4] Ring structure.

This is typical of political parties and voluntary organizations. Such structures can be described as follows:
Centre = president/CEO
Inner ring = secretary/treasurer/vice presidents etc.
+ presidents of committees for finance/membership/PR etc.
+ chairpersons of branches
Outer ring 1 = clusters of members of each committee
Outer ring 2 = clusters of members of each branch

In the outer rings the 'clusters' are like satellites (at the same radius) and each is another group of members which in turn holds local meetings and the committee presidents and branch chairpersons report back to the inner ring or *board* or *central committee.*

Thus committee chairpersons and branch presidents have to attend two lots of meetings, as will some branch members when these are delegates from the branches, as is often the case.

In the case of political parties the central committee is the elected members of the party in parliament. These 'politicians' often have to attend committee and branch meetings, as well as those of parliament, and are therefore often busier than we sometimes imagine.

Some additional aspects of such corporate structures are:

a. Hierarchical or 'one to one' structure as shown on the left in Figure 12.3.

b. A mixture of hierarchical and group structure is shown on the right in Figure 12.3.

c. Responsibilities of members may overlap, for example project manager A in Figure 12.2 is involved in two groups, that is with the group comprising the CEO and the other project managers and with the managers of the finance, HRM etc. divisions.

d. It is usually in the interests of middle level members that lower levels do not know the chain of command.

e. It is usually in the interests of both higher and lower levels that the chain of command is known.

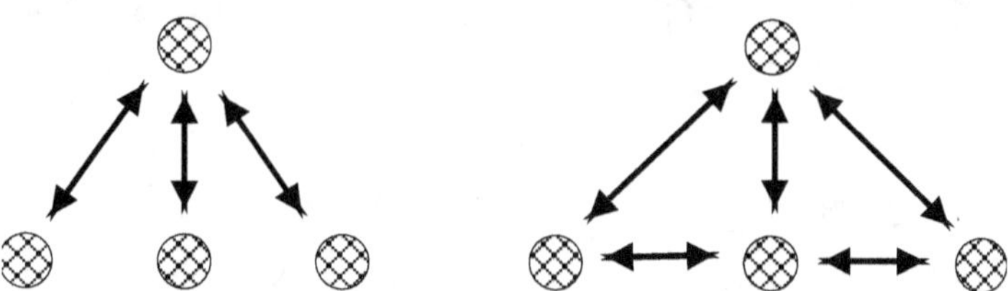

Figure 12.3. Hierarchical and group structures.

Generally, for example, case (b) is a more efficient structure than (a).

In case (d) middle level members are more empowered by ignorance of the chain of command by their subordinates. Whether this situation is in the interests of the company, however, is very doubtful and, indeed, it usually is not.

Such comments are merely a beginning in looking at the nuances of command structures. Further aspects of communication are considered elsewhere in the present book.

Finally, it should be noted that managers should be seeking to ensure that *effective communication* occurs throughout the corporate structure and it is not difficult to personally check that information has been properly passed on from time to time. That the information is understandable and is being given to people capable of understanding it is a matter that should also be given some consideration.

Business policy

The first goal of corporate thinking is to establish business policy (BP). Perhaps the four basic elements of business policy formulation are *environment, resources, constraints* and *objectives.*

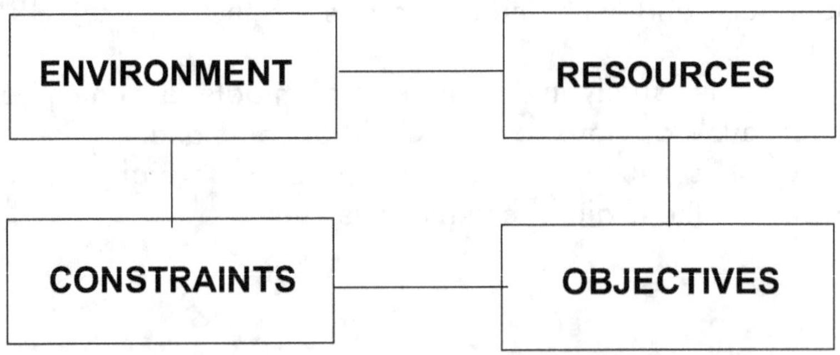

Figure 12.4. Fixed element analysis model.

These four elements are shown in the fixed element analysis model of Figure 12.4. With each of these there are both *qualitative* and *quantitative* matters to consider. Briefly considering each of these in turn:

Environment

Quantitative considerations include market size, scale of operations, capital requirements.

Qualitative considerations include who are the competitors in the marketplace, product differentiation, patents and product distribution.

Resources

Quantitative resources might include available finance, material and human resources.

Qualitative resources might include corporate strategy and tactics, a company structure and/or role model.

Constraints

Quantitative constraints will include finance limits, human limitations and resistance, material and human resource limits, and market size.

Qualitative constraints will include legal restrictions as well, of course, as union work restrictions.

Note that there are *internal constraints* such as work force size and *external constraints* such as laws.

Objectives

Quantitative objectives might include maximum sales and maximum profit.

Qualitative objectives might include good corporate image, customer loyalty, product quality, and personnel loyalty.

In this context the term *Management by Objectives* (MBO) is worth note and this simply refers to management styles which focus primarily on such objectives as the 'bottom line.'

Controllable element analysis

Once the fixed elements of Figure 12.4 are fully defined attention can turn to considering the controllable elements of business policy. These include:

- ➤ Corporate goals and objectives: these should include both short and long-term plans.
- ➤ Corporate structure: what is the most efficient structure for the company?
- ➤ Finance policies: target operating margins, profits and return on capital. Levels of debt and equity.
- ➤ HRM policies: types of people required and levels of remuneration.
- ➤ Manufacturing policies: location of plants and processes to be used.

➢ Marketing policies: product pricing and market positioning. Forms of advertising and advertising budget.
➢ Distribution policies: mode of distribution.
➢ Accounting policies.
➢ R&D policies: what percentage of profits will be put back into R&D? Are joint R&D ventures possible?

Once these business policies have been established they should be reexamined to check such things as:

[1] Is the company well enough differentiated from others in the same marketplace?

[2] Are the products well enough differentiated from competing products?

[3] Are the finance, marketing, distribution and other policies sufficient to ensure ongoing operations and adequate sales?

[4] Are there contingency plans should any problems occur?

Clearly establishing detailed business policy, therefore, is no easy matter and a good deal of thought is required, usually from a number of people in the case of a large organization.

Conclusions

The crucial thinking in setting up a company is formation of the four fixed elements of business policy. In order the major initial decisions are:
➢ Environment: product choice(s), marketing.
➢ Resources: finance, start-up personnel.
➢ Constraints: finance, personnel and time limitations.
➢ Objectives: initial break-even and thence survival.

In larger organizations an effective corporate structure is required to communicate business policy and maintain day-to-day operations.

Chapter 13

LEADERSHIP

People ask the difference between a leader and a boss.
The leader works in the open, and the boss in covert.
The leader leads, and the boss drives.
Theodore Roosevelt, speech 24 Oct. 1910, Binghamton N.Y.

Leadership

According to Bennis (1989), becoming a leader involves:

- Ongoing curiosity and learning.
- A motivational vision.
- Communicating that vision to inspire others to follow it.
- Being prepared to take risks.
- Maturity, honesty, and willingness to accept criticism.
- Searching for solutions to problems.
- Seeking success in small, incremental steps rather than waiting years for "Big Success".

In *The One Minute Manager* three keys to one minute management are proposed:

1. Agree on up to 6 goals with staff and put them in writing.

2. Staff should provide detailed records of progress to management.

3. When there is a lack of progress, management feedback should focus on any poor results, not the persons responsible, and should encourage staff to keep trying (Blanchard & Johnson, 1981).

Leadership and group performance

Formal communication within a company will tend to follow the corporate structure. Effective communication can considerably improve productivity and morale.

Figure 13.1 shows the results of a study of the relationship between mean or average performance (or productivity) and amount of contact with the group supervisor. Clearly relatively frequent and regular management contact improves productivity as we would expect (Mohr, 2014b, 2018d).

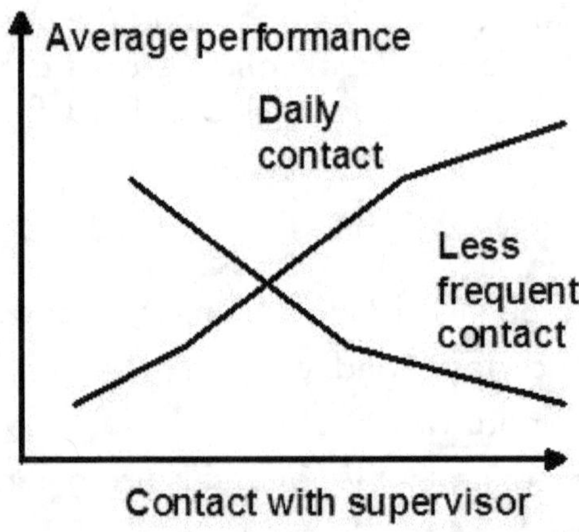

Figure 13.1. Communication with management.

Figure 13.2 shows the type of result obtained in a correlation of worker performance and group loyalty, indicating that productivity improves if group loyalty is high. In part this improvement results from the (necessary) emergence of 'team leadership'.

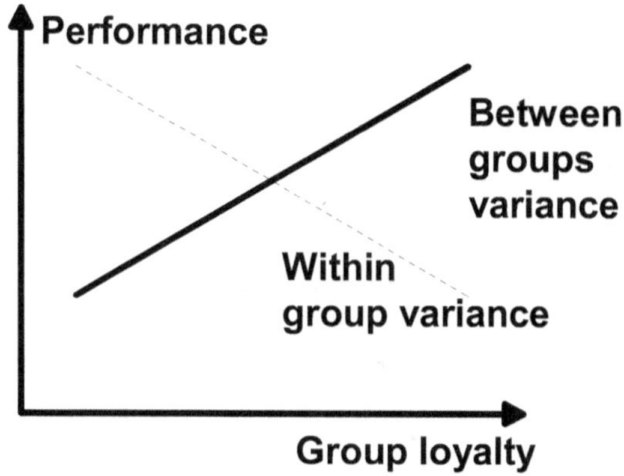

Figure 13.2. Performance and communication
with boss vs. group loyalty.

The study of Figure 13.2 also found that correlation between the proportion of workers who took their complaints to the boss and group loyalty took the same form (that shown).

In addition, the correlation between how easy the group found communication with the boss and group loyalty also took the same (ascending) form shown in Figure 13.2.

Effective communication (and hence loyalty) within the group and with the supervisor, therefore, both lead to improved productivity. In addition group loyalty improves communication with the supervisor, that is, the factors of group loyalty, amount of supervisor communication, quality of supervisor communication, and productivity are all interwoven in such a way as to suggest that if communication is optimized considerable improvements in productivity might result.

Figure 13.3 shows expected productivity compared to actual productivity for both the supervisor and the workers. Clearly the expectations of the supervisor are greater than those of the workers and are always fairly close to the target productivity.

The expectations of the workers, on the other hand, are for improvement when productivity is low and for slowing down when productivity is high, and are perhaps more realistic.

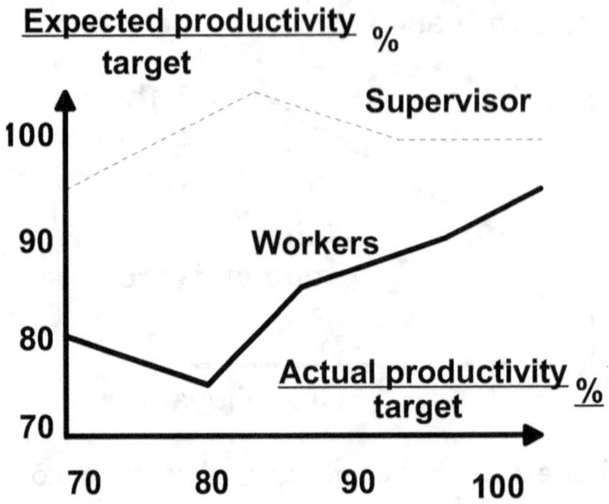

Figure 13.3. Expected vs. actual productivity

Unfortunately, however, there is no data from this study on the correlation between supervisor and worker expectations though this, of course, would depend on communications and, in any case, productivity variation is our main concern.

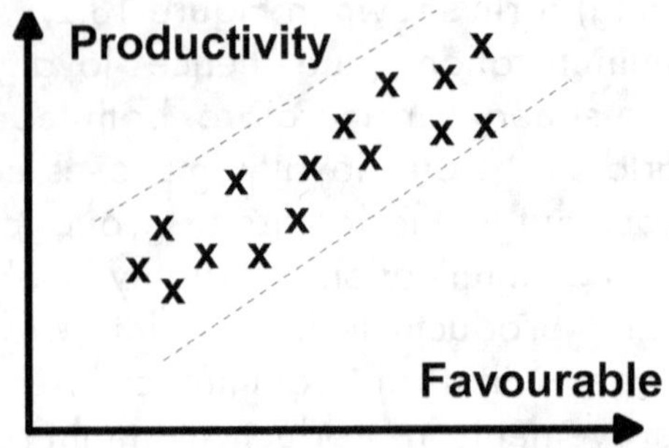

Figure 13.4. Dependence of productivity on supervisor attitude.

Figure 13.4 shows the results of a study of the effect of attitude of supervisor on productivity. There was a considerable spread in the results but there was sufficient correlation to support the finding that the more favourable the attitude of the supervisor (to both the workers and the job) the greater the productivity, as we might expect.

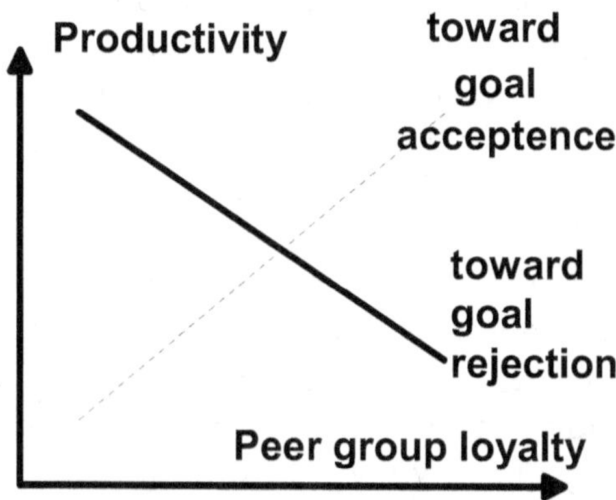

Figure 13.5. Loyalty towards company goals vs. productivity

We might also expect that favourable supervisor attitude resulted in more favourable worker attitude and that the latter also results in greater productivity.

Figure 13.5 shows the relationship of peer group loyalty to productivity when motivation is towards accepting versus rejecting company goals. Clearly peer group loyalty towards company goals results in greater productivity as we would expect.

The results of Figure 13.5 are related to those of Figure 13.2, showing that group loyalty is a very important factor in productivity.

Conclusion

Besides those conclusions already made in the foregoing discussion, the following recommendations are suggested as worthwhile by the results of Figures 13.1 – 13.5:

[1] There should be effective communication of productivity goals.

[2] There should be thorough assessment of productivity results.

[3] Groups and tasks with low productivity should be identified.

[4] Group loyalty should be encouraged and groups should be motivated to accept new staff and 'loners' in a group.

[5] Leadership audits should be used.
[6] Supervisors should exhibit favourable attitude and communicate frequently and regularly with their staff.
[7] Group loyalty toward company goals should be sought.
[8] Supervisors should make themselves freely available to staff with complaints and other feedback and make themselves easy to communicate with.

Generally, therefore, good leadership involving sufficient efficient communication of goals and team attitudes is likely to result in very considerable improvements in productivity.

It is also important, however, that measurements are made of productivity, group loyalty and management efficiency. The results will then be useful in identifying problems requiring correction and productivity results when favourable, for example, can be used as motivational information for supervisors and their groups (Mohr, 2014b, 2018d).

As shown in Figs 13.1 to 13.5 effective communication that improves productivity will:
[1] Be regular.
[2] Promote communication and thence loyalty between workers.
[3] Communicate realistic production targets.
[4] Project a positive management attitude to both the work and the workers.
[5] Promote worker loyalty to the company and thence acceptance of company goals.

As a bottom line, developing detailed business policy requires a lot of thought and the ongoing operation of a company requires a good deal of communication and, in turn, much thought about feedback etc.

Chapter 14

MOHR'S LAW OF HIERARCHIES

All inequality that has no special utility to justify it is injustice.
Jeremy Bentham, Supply Without Burthen or Escheat Vice Taxation,
Jeremy Bentham's Economic Writings (W. Stark, ed., 1952).

Detestation of the high is the involuntary homage of the low.
Charles Dickens, *A Tale of Two Cities* (1859).

The Peter Principle

Dr Laurence Peter drew on his experiences in the education sector to try and explain why we always seem to have lousy leaders (Peter & Hull, 1969). The result was his celebrated *Peter Principle*:

> ### In a hierarchy every employee tends to rise to his own level of incompetence.

In other words, *the sour cream rises.*

A corollary is: *In time every post tends to be occupied by an employee who is incompetent to carry out his duties.*

In his often tongue-in-cheek book Peter gives a few excellent historical examples of his celebrated principle, including:

(a) Socrates was a brilliant philosopher but a lousy defence attorney.

(b) Hitler was a brilliant politician but a lousy general.

Mohr's Law of Hierarchies

This can illustrated by the small (hierarchical) DC network shown in Figure 14.1 which can be modeled as a DC network using a simple Finite Element Method program given in Chapter 23 (Mohr, 1992, 2012a, 2018e).

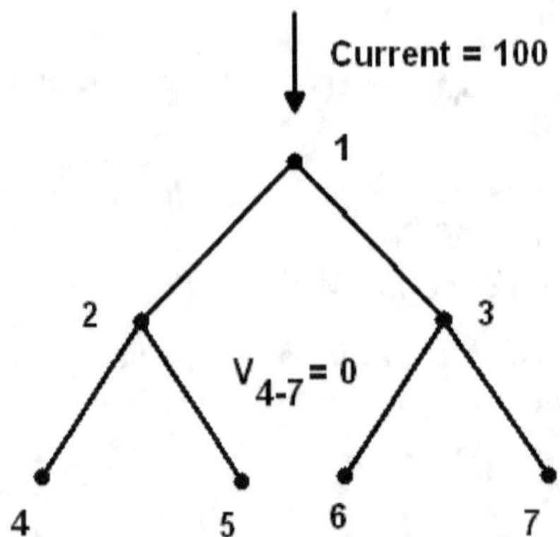

Figure 14.1. Hierarchical network.

At node 1 we have the pyramid building and lunatic 'boss' and a current 'load' of 100 is input. This is done by specifying the voltage at node 1 as 100, this being equivalent to adding a 'load' to the network.

Then zero datum voltage is specified at nodes 4-7 and unit resistance is given to all 6 elements so that the results from the program are:

Voltage 75 at node 1.
Voltage 25 at nodes 2 and 3.
Zero voltage at nodes 4 to 7.
Currents 50 in the top two elements and 25 in the rest.

This illustrates what the 'econobabble' of economists and politicians calls 'the trickledown effect', that is, the boss of this very small hierarchy has 3 times the voltage (or power, money and status) of his subordinates (the front line managers) one rung below. The workers at the bottom have no status at all.

If we add a further bottom row of 8 nodes in Figure 14.1 then now the 'voltage hierarchy' is 87.5, 37.5, 12.5, 0 so that the boss now does 7 times as well as the 'front line managers' on the row above the bottom row.

Then if we add a further fifth row of 16 nodes the voltage hierarchy is 93.75, 43.75, 18.75, 6.25, 0 and the boss does 15 times as well as the front line managers and infinitely better than the workers at the bottom!

The latter 'voltage hierarchy' is the fundamental principle of modern management, leading to Mohr's Law of Hierarchies:

In hierarchical organizations the amount of real material-producing work people do is inversely proportional to their rank or level in the organization.
The amount of compensation they receive, however, is proportional to their level, sometimes to an exponential degree.

For such people their earnings might be expressed as an exponential function: $\$ = C\exp(kR)$

where $\$$ = salary, R = rank, and C and k are constants.

This, of course, is not fair at all.

In ancient times philosophers felt that nobody should be paid more than about 10 or 20 times as much as anybody else, and even that is a great difference, of course, but it might be justified in the case of an elected national leader who must be able to present a strong, powerful image and might have only a relatively short term in office.

In the case of big business, however, things have got out of hand and remuneration of CEOs is often tens of millions, on top of which they get huge share issues as annual bonuses, huge 'golden handshakes' when they retire, and gigantic 'golden parachutes' then the company collapses.

To add insult to the injury of poverty, the worker-slaves endure 'top-down one-way' (TDOW) communication as they did all through their long years at school, in other words, they are treated like shit.

This is grossly unjust as the poor peasants who work on farms, in factories or on building sites produce what is essential to human life, that is, food, clothing, housing etc.

So those posters often seen in the USSR decades ago which pictured the workers as heroic perhaps made some sense. Then, of course, the hammer and sickle on their flag was also symbolic of the importance of the workers.

So the bottom line is that we have to create fairer societies which have real or *direct democracy* and leaders who 'check their ego at the door'. In these greed, hunger, famine, war and other evils will not be tolerated by the people.

Power corrupts

As figure 14.1 illustrates, the higher up you are in a hierarchy the more 'power' you have, which might be stated symbolically as:

$$P = C R^n$$

where P = power, R = rank, and C and n are constants.

Assuming the value of n is 2 then when one is twice as high in the hierarchy one has four times as much power.

Then, as we all know, power corrupts, one of the major factors in mankind's endless history of conflict.

As noted in the previous section, salaries may increase exponentially in hierarchical organizations and this result can be related to Mohr's Law of Capitalism which is the exponential growth law of money (\$) with time (T)

$$d(\$)/d(T) = c_1(\text{activity}) \quad \text{where activity} = c_2 \$$$

Here the rate at which money is made is proportional to the rate of business activity, this in turn proportional to the amount of money available to fund this activity.

Combining the two constants above as $k = c_1 c_2$ we have

$$d(\$)/d(T) = k\$ \quad \text{where } k \text{ is the } growth\ factor.$$

where \$ = money made.

This last equation is *separable* which means that it can be integrated in the form

Integral [d($)/$] = Integral [k d(T)]

giving, with the inclusion of the initial values, the exponential growth law $/$_0 = exp[k(T − T_0]

If, for example, the growth factor is 10% per year, that is k = 0.1, then over 10 years we obtain the growth ratio $/$_0 = 2.7, so that we have nearly *tripled* our money.

The only real beneficiaries, however, are those higher in the hierarchy. The workers at the bottom who do all the *real work* (sitting and raving at sometimes boozy board meetings is not hard work) can't usually save any money and thus are slaves to all intents and purposes.

This is an intolerable situation and the CEOs who earn 'megabucks' are, of course, corrupt, and such corruption has always sown the seeds of discontent that have always, sooner or later, ended up as revolutions.

Thus socialism tends to be ruled by a single dictator, but capitalism by a multiplicity of petty dictators:

Capitalism tends to produce a multiplicity of petty dictators each in command of his own little business kingdom. State Socialism tends to produce a single, centralized totalitarian dictatorship, wielding absolute authority . . . through a hierarchy of bureaucratic agents.
Aldous Huxley, *Ends and Means* (1937).

Politicians too are often corrupt, of course, often being found to take bribes from big business.

Monarchs and dictators, of course, have nearly always been the greediest of all. Not only do they help themselves to plenty of money and live in grand palaces, but throughout history their hunger for power and thence territorial gain has led to one war after another.

Conclusion

Hierarchies are difficult to deal with over the long term.

When one is young, and not long out of the education system, they are simply a learning experience at first. Over time, however, grudges over being treated badly, and impatience over lack of promotion, grow and grow to the point at which getting another job may seem the only hope of improving one's life and career prospects.

If one has a psychopathic 'bastard boss', however, it may be impossible to get a halfway supportive reference from them, without which getting a decent job, or any job at all in line with your abilities, qualifications and experience, may prove difficult.

In this way, indeed, just one bad boss can ruin your life, and in the first author's unfortunate case, two almost successive and too young/aggressive/alpha-male and inexperienced and boozing bastard bosses did, in fact, ruin his University career (Mohr, 2018e).

Some of the concepts and suggestions made in the foregoing chapter may be of some help, however, to workers with bad bass problems.

For example, remembering the Peter Principle will help one see the lighter side of the problem, while some of the suggestions made on how to diagnose and deal with psychopathic bosses might at least give the reader a few ideas from which he might be able to construct a strategy for dealing with a bad boss.

Primarily, of course, one needs at least one or two helpers within the organization in question. A problem here is that the workers at the same level in the hierarchy are also competing for the same promotion that you are. Thus, if you are in a group of, say, 10 seeking promotion to 'Senior xyz', then one might establish a mutually supportive relationship with just one of them, hoping that you will both be the next two workers promoted.

Chapter 15

DEALING WITH BAD BOSSES

I'm the boss. I'm allowed to yell.
Ivan Boesky, q. in *Den of* Thieves, James B Stewart, 1991.

In every one of those little stucco boxes there's some poor bastard
who's never free except when he's fast asleep
and dreaming that he's got the boss down the bottom
of a well and is bunging lumps of coal at him.
George Orwell, *Coming Up For Air,* pt 1., ch. 2 (1939).

How hierarchies operate

Hierarchies operate through a chain of command, leaders meeting with a chosen few top-level executives responsible for overseeing the various operations of the organization. In the case of government, for example, there are ministers for defence, treasury, education, health, and so forth.

In each of these areas there is a permanent and hierarchical bureaucratic department with several levels of seniority ranging from head of the organization and department heads to front-line managers who manage teams of workers.

Through the whole chain of command there is an implicit level of intimidation and fear that usually makes sure that everybody does as they are told. At the front line, however, things often get ridiculous, for example the traditional screaming of army sergeants at their miserable subordinates.

It is through such bullying and intimidation, of course, that soldiers are brainwashed into following orders without question or delay, essentially becoming expendable slaves to satisfy the whims of their leaders. Don't worry about 'executive stress,' therefore, worry about 'slave-stress.'

Indeed, our many sports with a relationship to conflict, for example absurd rugby with its 'charge at the enemy' no matter what the risk of injury, or archery and rifle shooting, all relate to our historical predilection for conflict.

Throughout hierarchies there is, of course, ambition to rise, often leading to a good deal of competitive behaviour, much of it often downright dishonest and unfair. In politics, for example, plenty of 'backstabbing' goes on day in and day out.

This corresponds quite closely, perhaps, with the alpha-male behaviour seen in several animal species, notably our close relatives, gorillas. The result is, of course, that those who end up as leaders may well be the most rotten people in the organization and, indeed, historically in both government and business this has always proved to be the case to some extent at least. That is, leaders are always greedy and bossy to some extent at least, but often they are exceptionally so.

Within hierarchical organizations there is also conflict, particularly over the 'rat race' involved in rising in the hierarchy.

Indeed, often ambitious, driven people are psychopathic, the pathology of their condition involving lying, cheating, aggressiveness, and bullying to get to the top.

Given power, it seems, they become psychotic with dreams of greater wealth and power and thus superiority. Alexander the Great, for example, began to think that he must be divine.

The problem is that, being people who have proved themselves good at the 'rat race', they tend to be the worst leaders, exactly in accordance with the Peter Principle.

Not only that, power not only corrupts, it makes people vain, self-centred, neurotic, obsessive, and, basically, mad. Here we must hasten to note Mohr's 10th Law, that is, that things such as madness must be judged on a scale of 1 to 10, not merely as a true-or-false judgment.

Furthermore, we like to make the important distinction between *bad mad* (depression etc.) and *sad mad* (Mohr, 2012b, 2018c; Mohr et al., 2018), and all too often political leaders have been bad mad, for example Nero and Hitler.

Diagnosing psychopaths

Table 15.1. The Hare checklist for psychopaths.

	TRAIT	SCORE
	Facet 1: Interpersonal	
1	Glibness or superficial charm	1
2	Grandiose sense of self-worth	1
3	Pathological lying	2
4	Cunning or manipulative	1
	Facet 2: Affective	
5	Lack of remorse or guilt	1
6	Emotionally shallow	1
7	Callous or lack of empathy	1
8	Failure to accept responsibility for their own actions	1
	Facet 3: Lifestyle	
9	Need for stimulation (easily bored)	1
10	Parasitic lifestyle	1
11	Lack of realistic, long-term goals	0
12	Impulsivity	1
13	Irresponsibility	0
	Facet 4: Antisocial	
14	Poor behavioural controls	0
15	Early behavioural problems	0
16	Juvenile delinquency	0
17	History of conditional prison release being revoked	0
18	Criminal versatility	0
	Other traits:	
19	Many short-term marital relationships	0
20	Promiscuous sexual behaviour	0
TOTAL SCORE		**12**

In 1980, Canadian clinical psychologist Dr Robert Hare, who worked in prisons, released the first version of the Hare checklist for identifying psychopaths, and several further versions followed.

As shown in Table 15.1, it divides 20 personality traits into four groups: interpersonal, affective, lifestyle, and antisocial, these measuring traits including charm, propensity to lie, lack of remorse, and need for stimulation.

After an interview each trait is scored as 0 (not present), 1 (present but not dominant), or 2 (dominant), so that the maximum possible score is 40.

Average people score from 3 to 6, non-psychopathic criminals score from 16 to 22, whilst in the UK and US respectively, scores of >25 and >30 are taken as a positive diagnosis of psychopathy (Gillespie, 2017).

The first author has scored a couple of bad bosses he once had, both of whom were too young and inexperienced for being HOD, and played a major role in destroying his promising University career when he was less than 40.

Their total score of 12 seemed too low, as both seemed at least somewhat psychopathic, suggesting that Table 15.1 might apply more to hardened criminals for which item 17 relates to a form of 'treatment', namely continued imprisonment, presumably because of little or no sign of rehabilitation or remorse. Similarly, items 16 and 19 relate to past history.

Thus criteria for judging a bad boss should include:
➢ Bossiness.
➢ Assertiveness.
➢ Dishonesty and lying.
➢ Selfishness and greed.
➢ Vanity.
➢ Bullying.

Dealing with psychopaths

Gillespie (2017) suggests that organizations which are run using 'Management by Objectives' (MBO) are conducive to psychopathic bosses:

"The only way for a psychopath to succeed in a structure based on MBO would be to fall in with the objectives of his team and his superiors. Anything else would mark him out for removal from the organization."

Alternatively, Gillespie suggests that persons deemed to be psychopaths can be got rid of by getting them 'fired', but this, of course, is very difficult to bring about when the only person in the part of the organization in question able to do firing is a psychopathic boss, as is often the case.

When you do go above his or her head seeking to get them fired they counterattack, usually resulting in the person or persons complaining being disciplined or fired.

Most workers, therefore, simply have to endure bad and mad bosses and a 2016 study of Australian workplaces with "toxic leaders" concluded that the following strategies were unwise (Gillespie, 2017):

➢ Confronting the leader.
➢ Avoiding, ignoring or bypassing the boss.
➢ Whistleblowing.
➢ Worrying to excess about the boss.
➢ Continued anger and frustration.
➢ Focusing on work to try and forget about the boss.
➢ Taking sick leave (giving only short-term relief).

Instead, Gillespie says one should behave as a polite and compliant employee and do whatever one is told, no matter how much one dislikes it. Then to survive in this way one should also:

➢ Think about a future, better job.
➢ Make sure your fellow workers don't 'tell' on each other.
➢ Check the accuracy of what the boss says.
➢ Don't show any anger and frustration.
➢ Build a support network.
➢ Document every bad thing the boss does, noting the time, date and names of any witnesses.

In this way one can survive for the medium term, at least, and perhaps build a case against the bad boss that might result in him being disciplined, demoted or shifted sideways, or even fired.

A case study

Many a career, indeed life, has been ruined by a bad boss, the first author being a good example, having had the misfortune of having two inexperienced, too young for the job, etcetera, HODs in the Engineering faculties of Universities in Melbourne and Auckland. In both cases, despite in the end having done far more work, research and writing than both bad bosses, he was simply too low in the hierarchy to survive.

His main mistake was focusing too hard on publishing as many research papers as possible in international journals, and trying to get a gradually growing scientific textbook out, having been mucked around badly by one publisher over it for years.

In the end he resigned meekly when the new Auckland HOD offered to have him paid 4 months in advance to pay for me to return himself and family to Melbourne.

In fact, he should have had this somewhat illegal offer put in writing, and taken that, along with complaints about his having bullied him a few times, for example by saying: " - - Engineers are stupid" (the new HOD he was a mathematician, the first author was an engineer) to the Dean.

Then he could have insisted that some action disciplinary action be taken, and that a minor promotion that the nasty boss had held up for a couple of years on the basis of obvious lies (which were in writing) be finally granted.

The bottom line, therefore, is that alone and miserably underpaid he felt worn down by pressure over a period of years, and simply 'walked the plank', when, in fact, he should have sought help to deal with the problem.

He should also have used the questionnaire given in the following chapter, one which he had used to have students rate him as a lecturer compared to the first of two bad bosses a few years earlier. This may well have again rated him better than the new HOD, proving that he was not a "lousy lecturer" as the new HOD had said in the corridor one day.

The bottom line, of course, is that there is a lesson to be learnt by any reader from this, namely having problems with a bad boss, give plenty of thought and get as much help as needed to deal with the problem and, hopefully, resolve it somehow, whether that help was simply support from one or two other staff members, or help from people above the bad boss in the hierarchy, and, if need be, lawyers.

Conclusions

With the recent rise of the ME TO movement, bullying in the workplace has, like sexual abuse in the Catholic Church, become a prominent issue.

In dealing with a bad boss it helps to:

- Identify any psychopathic behaviours of the boss.
- Try to speak carefully to the boss about the problems, perhaps with a friend or colleague to back you up.
- Get as much as possible from the bad boss in writing.
- Consider recording bad behavior somehow.
- Ask advice from friends and family about any problems.
- Go above the bad boss in the hierarchy about problems.
- Speak to counselors and perhaps lawyers about problems.
- Consider using a simple person scaling survey such as that given in the following chapter to get a 'rating' of the bad boss which might then be given to people higher in the hierarchy.

The bottom line, however, is that one should ignore bullying, threats etc. from bad bosses, but make careful records of such behavior and seek help in dealing with the issue, being careful to behave at a professional and courteous manner at all times, hoping not to exacerbate the situation, but to resolve it as well as possible, and to the benefit of all parties.

Chapter 16

PERSON SCALING

Opinions are to the vast apparatus of social existence what oil is to machines: one does not go up to a turbine and pour machine oil over it; one applies a little to hidden spindlesand joints that one has to know.
Walter Benjamin, One-Way Street, "Filling Station" (1928).

Introduction

As suggested in the previous chapter, 'person scaling' can be used to evaluate the performance and/or behavior of a boss that is giving you problems, and one can also apply the same survey to oneself for comparison. Indeed, the first author (GAM) used the survey given in the present chapter to assess the performance of both himself and a new and bad boss at the Caulfield Campus of Monash University, but made no use of it.

At first this did not matter because he moved to Auckland University, appointed by a HOD about to retire. Again the new HOD was too young and inexperienced for the job, and had simply not done enough in his career to sit back and play HOD.

The result was that when a colleague verbally attacked GAM one day, having been encouraged to do so by the ex-HOD back in Melbourne, he complained to the new HOD in Auckland, who took sides against him and also bullied him, and held up an approved promotion.

As noted in the 'case study' of the previous chapter, GAM eventually resigned under pressure, never to get another job because bad boss wrote him backstabbing confidential references, whilst the ex-bad boss in Melbourne was too nasty to even use as a referee.

In hindsight, it might have been good idea to use the survey questionnaire of Table 16.1 to again assess the bad HOD's performance, and compare it to his own. This would probably have rated the bad HOD as a worse lecturer than GAM, and the results could have been shown to the Dean, telling him that the bad HOD had called him/GAM a "lousy lecturer" in just one bullying episode of many.

Hopefully, however, others might learn from this 'lesson', and perhaps find a survey such as that given here useful.

Person scaling

Unlike stimulus-person scaling techniques, person scaling techniques make no attempt to locate responses on a scale and they are classified *a priori* as either favourable or unfavourable toward the attitude object. Then the location of persons on the attitude dimension is determined by the number of stimuli with which they agree and the extent of their agreement.

These person scaling methods are derivatives of the psychometric model traditionally much used for ability or IQ tests in which responses to items are viewed as indicators of a common latent ability.

Likert's *method of summated ratings* was designed to be much easier to use than the method of equal-appearing intervals but to be at least as reliable. In this approach a large pool of items which are chosen intuitively for their relevance to the attitude object is used. These items usually consist of statements of belief, but statements about behaviours or affective reactions can also be used.

Typically, in Likert scaling each item is presented to respondents in a multiple-choice format such as:

1. Strongly disagree.
2. Disagree.
3. Undecided.
4. Agree.
5. Strongly agree.

Then the response to each item is given a score such as 5 for strongly agree.

Then, for example, a survey on attitudes towards women might contain questions like:

(a) Swearing is more objectionable from a woman.

(b) Intoxication in women is worse than in men.

With scores from 1 - 5 given to each of perhaps a dozen or so such questions the total score is then obtained for each respondent.

For best results an initial 'pool' of items can be pilot tested on a group of people to eliminate ambiguous and nondiscriminating items which tend to result in neutral responses. This can be done by examining the *item-total score correlations*, each of which correlates the respondents' scores on an item with their scores summed over all the items. Then a good item will have a positive correlation and generally better items have higher correlations.

Example of Likert scaling

The following table gives an example of a type of questionnaire which the fist author found useful over two decades ago for class evaluation of teaching. Students enjoyed the revenge [in advance] of giving a mark out of 100, especially as they were asked to also give marks (with different colour pen or ringed etc.) to the HOD who shared teaching of the subject with him. The HOD cored pretty badly!

Though it looks a little formidable this survey worked well and gave the desired results which, however, were never used.

Table 16.1. Questionnaire using Likert scaling.

Circle the appropriate number:	Very good	Good	Aver-age	Fair	Poor
Rate your lecturer's:					
1. Choice of material	5	4	3	2	1
2. Performance generally	5	4	3	2	1
3. Explanations of the theory	5	4	3	2	1
4. Use of practical examples	5	4	3	2	1
5. Development of theory	5	4	3	2	1
6. Stressing important points	5	4	3	2	1
7. Choice of tutorial examples	5	4	3	2	1
8. Time given to individuals	5	4	3	2	1
9. Choice of lab. experiments	5	4	3	2	1
10. Helping understand subject	5	4	3	2	1
11. Useful in its own right	5	4	3	2	1
12. Teaching report writing	5	4	3	2	1
How well does the lecturer do in:					
13. Getting you interested	5	4	3	2	1
14. Knowledge of subject	5	4	3	2	1
15. Motivating you	5	4	3	2	1
16. Giving clear explanations	5	4	3	2	1
17. Lecturing at followable rate	5	4	3	2	1
18. Giving good lecture notes	5	4	3	2	1
Other:					
19. Are the tests useful?	5	4	3	2	1
20. Course relevant to needs?	5	4	3	2	1
Add the numbers you circled:	**Score/100:**				

In other contexts, such a survey about a bad boss might ask questions about their behavior, communication, politeness etc.

Pareto's Law

Pareto's Law (Slaybaugh, 1967) is:

In most situations a relatively small percentage of certain objects contributes a relatively high percentage of output.

This is the basis of *contribution-by-value analysis* (also called ABC analysis).

For instance 15-30 percent of the population contributes 70-90 percent of the tax revenue, 20 percent of the employees in an office may do 60 percent of the work, or 20 percent of the items in inventory may account for 60 percent of the sales.

As an example of ABC analysis, the percentage of total dollar annual sales for each product are calculated and tabulated in descending order. Then the cumulative percentage contribution is added as a final column to show how much, say, the first 20% of products contributes.

The point of mentioning Pareto's Law here is that a survey questionnaire could sensibly be used to rate a group of people in a workplace to find out which ones are more productive.

Conclusion

A person scaling questionnaire such as that of the example given in Table 16.1 could be used for many purposes other than the usual one of market research, for example to get a relatively negative assessment of bad bass, which might be helpful in dealing improving a bad situation.

The same questionnaire can also be used, of course, to get a more positive assessment of oneself, which might also be of considerable help in dealing with workplace problems.

16. Person Scaling.

PART IV
HOME LIFE

Chapter 17

FINDING A PARTNER

Wisest men
Have erred, and by bad women been deceived;
And shall again, pretend they ne'er so wise.
John Milton, *Samson Agonistes* 1, 210 (1671).

Introduction

In the old days boys meeting girls with a view to learning about the opposite sex was harder to do, especially if one went to a single sex school. Then dances run for teenagers were just about the only formal opportunity for 'research' so that it was not highly uncommon for a man to end up marrying a girl from the same or a nearby school, or who lived in the same street, or who even lived next door.

These days there are youth centres for school-age children to meet up to five days a week and also at regular special functions.

Once one reaches 18 there are pubs and clubs, of course, and even Internet and phone services advertised on late-night TV that introduce lonely people.

Today, of course, younger people often share flats and houses and, of course, that is a way of meeting the opposite sex. Indeed, it is my experience more than once that advertising a room in a house is a quite likely way of finding a friend and women know this full well. They are fully aware of the possible consequences of living in the same abode as another man and, indeed, often seek to meet a man in this way.

Love at first sight?

When a single person looking for a partner meets a person of the opposite sex they should try to form a sound opinion of the person by considering such factors as:
- Looks.
- Body language. This is especially important including how does it feel to have the person close to you?
- Personality.
- Do they seem relaxed or nervous meeting you?
- Do they seem genuinely pleased to meet you?
- Their age, occupation and educational background.
- Have they been single for long? If so, why?
- Where did their parents come from?
- What do her parents do?

This is quite a lot of data to gather and it may take more than one meeting to acquire it. At the first meeting a kiss or hug or two is OK but nothing more than that should be considered. If either person is too drunk to care about this limitation then that should end the first meeting. If polite refusal causes offence that is good reason to end the first meeting and never have another one.

If a second meeting is had that allows time to complete the foregoing data list and assess the person and also assess your own feelings for the person. The second meeting, however, is still too soon to sensibly consider having sex with the person.

Further research

On meeting the new person for the second and subsequent times it may be useful to consider how both they and you rate in terms of the 'CAB' response illustrated in Figure 21.1.

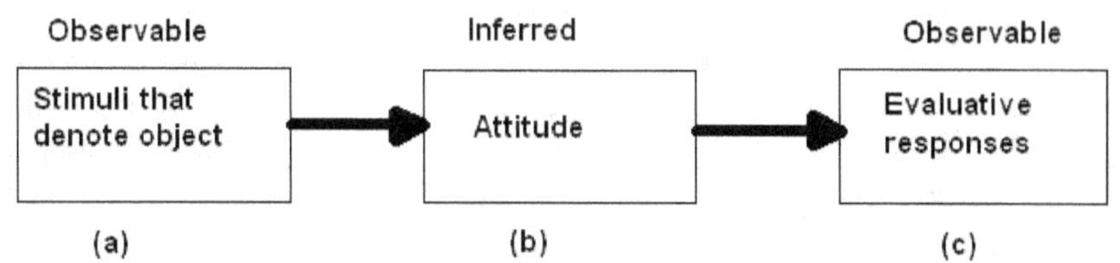

Figure 21.1. Cognitive, attitudinal, and behavioural responses.

Here Figure 21.1 illustrates the three types of response involved in attitudinal psychology (Eagly & Chaiken, 1993). These are:

1. *Cognitive response* or recognition of a stimulus, in this case seeing the person again.
2. *Affective response* or the feelings or emotions this recognition gives you..
3. *Behavioural response* or what you think you would now like to do.

Evaluating your response to a new acquaintance is important, as is estimating what you think their response to you is. In both cases the cognitive response should be instant recognition, followed by facial expressions and body language that indicate attitude, and finally behaviour such as, for example, turning away from you which, of course, is probably a sure sign of negative feelings.

If things go so far as meeting two or three times you should be in a position to make a decision table to evaluate the new friend and thus decide whether to continue the relationship for a significant period.

Table 21.1. Decision table.

Attribute	Scores/10	
	Person A	Person B
Looks		
Body language		
Personality		
Talkative		
Apparent IQ		
Family background		
Education		
Occupation		
Honesty (perceived)		
Good worker?		
Generous		
Friends or a loner?		
Sex OK		
TOTAL		

Table 21.1 is a decision table comparing the attributes of two people using Likert Scaling (Likert 1961; Eagly & Chaiken 1993). Obviously if one has a much better score than the other then that might suggest them as a better partner for a long-term relationship.

Believe it or not, a woman I once met when divorced put me under a tiny bit of pressure on the commitment issue and I responded by suggesting such a table. She duly compiled one and in the column for me the score for sex was blanked out, perhaps mercifully!

On a more serious note, communication depends in part sometimes in what two people have in common to talk about, for example, what to have for dinner, or their children. At the beginning of a relationship, however, it is far more important to assess whether there is much in your respective personal and family backgrounds to talk about.

Do you for example, have similar tastes in music, literature and sport? Are you both the 'arty' or the scientific types? And so on, but very important.

Communication will also depend, in part at least, on intelligence. When you talk about a certain subject does the other person sometimes quickly respond with new information or a useful suggestion? If so, that is a sign of intelligence.

Jencks et al. (1975) report that men with IQs of 120 have wives with an average IQ of 111 and that wives with an IQ of 120 have husbands with an average IQ of 111.

Thus they have not married randomly for, had they done so, their partners would have an average IQ of 100.

Living together

The decision whether or not to live together should be based on data such as that required for Table 21.1 and, of course, should not be made in haste.

Only a few decades ago unmarried men and women living together were deemed to be living in sin and whether or not to get married usually took years to decide.

This has changed greatly but still the decision on whether to live in a de facto marriage situation should not be taken lightly and only after the relationship has lasted at least a few months without problems:

I have only ever refused to marry one couple,
and that was because they had only just met.
The whole thing sounded good in theory. There simply hadn't
been enough time for the process of deliberation.
I told them that if they wanted to get married, they could go to a
registry office and in a month's time they would be husband and
wife but, If they wanted me to do the ceremony, come back and
see me in four or five months and we would see how they were
getting on.
Within a couple of weeks their relationship was over.
Philip Baker, *Decisions of Daring Achievers* (2004).

When a couple do decide to live together that is only a beginning of sorts. Presumably sex has been tried out a good deal before cohabiting, hopefully with effective contraceptive measures in place. Such measures should continue, of course, until the relationship has lasted for, preferably, a few years.

At that point the relationship can be carefully reassessed and a decision made as to whether it should be continued, perhaps with the help of opinions and advice from friends and relatives.

If so, the question of children might be considered, but only after careful thought and planning, including careful consideration of whether the job and financial prospects of one, if not both, partners are secure for the long term.

On the important question of children advice is essential from friends, relatives and preferably a professional counselor, the bottom line being that marriage and relationship guidance counselors are needed before marriage, and most certainly before having children, not when the marriage strikes problems.

Indeed, independent advisors can consider the physical, emotional, and financial conditions of the relationship and thus take a 'potential child's' point of view in deciding whether it should be had.

Similarly, I would urge couples with children considering breaking up to be more democratic and consider their children's view of the matter also.

Chapter 18

FAMILY PLANNING

Half of all pregnancies in Britain are unplanned.
One in five will end in termination.
Statement issued by the alliance of FPA, BCT,
Brook Advisory Centres and the Health Education Authority,
1988, quoted in *The Whole Woman,* Greer (1999).

Introduction

All too often, even before a couple has decided to live together, pregnancy occurs and this may force the issue. This is an unfortunate situation that should be avoided at all costs because it puts great pressure on the relationship from the beginning. Instead of the couple getting to know each other and building a secure relationship and financial situation over a period of a few years, those early years are dominated by the unexpected demands and expenses of a child.

In the old days this situation was often the beginning of a lifelong poverty trap and these days it is often likely to result in the couple separating after a few years, a tragic result for all concerned, especially children.

Research has found that, as might be expected, children given more resources and attention, especially from the outset, do better at school and in later life.

Thus would-be parents owe it to their children to plan for them as well as possible.

Planning to have children

Considerable thought should be given to choosing a partner for a long-term relationship. Then the decision as to whether to live together (and get married at that point or later) should only be taken on the basis of advice from friends and relatives, and then only after the relationship has lasted at least a few months, preferably a year or two.

Living together already suggests the possibility of children, but that step should only be considered when the relationship is financially and emotionally secure, and on the basis of further advice and perhaps professional counseling.

Planning for the first child should include consideration of whether one's home is suitable for a child, whether at least one of the parents-to-be has a secure career, and whether the relationship is happy, stable and likely to be permanent.

Financial security is very important too, of course, and one should not consider having children unless one is in a secure financial position. Preferably, for example, one would already have bought one's own apartment or house and be able to manage the mortgage repayments of that as well as the increased living expenses that a child will bring.

The appearance of 'the pill' in the 1960s has, of course, made the task of family planning a great deal easier and Caro and Fox (2008) feel that the pill and tampon freed women considerably.

In addition, we now have the 'morning after' pill and the pill for men is in the research and development pipeline.

How many children?

The question of how many children a couple should have is, of course, a very important one.

In Victorian times in England families had between five and seven children but by the 1960s this had declined to just over two (Worsley, 1970). Indeed, circa 1960 my father said he believed in "ZPG" (zero population growth) and thence 2-child families, and the world would now be a much better place if that had, indeed, happened.

Less than a century ago large families were still common but now, in an overpopulated world with real living standards decreasing in the West, that is not an option for most people. Ordinary working people simply cannot afford it and rich people are usually careful not to have too many children and thus 'dilute' the family wealth.

China had an effective one child policy in place for a few decades and, indeed, only children are usually more intelligent, in part, of course, because they receive more care and attention (Vernon, 1960).

Weiss and Mann (1978), for example, refer to a project in Milwaukee that found that children given more attention by the mother or a specially trained teacher, showed markedly higher IQ.

Two children is, of course, a sensible number for those that can afford it. Both should be able to receive sufficient attention and resources to ensure a good upbringing.

A female relative of mine had a son, and then a second son not long after. Wanting a girl, I suspect with some urging from her own mother, she had a third child which was a girl. Indeed, she had taken some strange but doubtful measures to make having a girl more likely.

Then, hoping to balance the numbers, she had a fourth and last child but that turned out to be a boy. In the end four children in about 6 years really proved too much for them to deal with in terms of attention and discipline and two of the four children had serious problems with drugs, one of them ending up a hopeless schizophrenic mess.

Myself, having had two children and been divorced, I was fortunate to escape one marriage when the woman had a miscarriage. I escaped a second time when a woman became pregnant but was told the child would be "mildly retarded." Consulting experts I found that this really meant quite severe retardation and this information persuaded the woman to have an abortion at five months, perhaps a good example of how important it is to get advice sometimes.

Working mothers

If a family has only one or two children the mother, especially if she has a professional career for which she did years of training, may want to return to the workforce when at least one of the children are still young.

This will require the use of a day care centre and this is quite expensive, costing around $100 per day at present in Australia.

This cost usually comes out of post-tax earnings so that the cost of having two children in day care can easily erode most of a woman's wages, some women reporting that they earn as little as $50 a week after childcare is deducted.

At this point, of course, many women opt out of the workforce and become housewives.

As Bryson (1992) points out, from a social point of view, indeed, a woman staying at home caring for her children is making her contribution:

Marx and Engels did say that reproduction as well as production was a part of the material basis of society. In the 'German Ideology' they wrote of "the production of life, both of one's own in labour and of fresh life in procreation."

In addition, stay at home mothers may be in a better position to give their children a head start in learning, a matter discussed further in Chapter 24.

Conclusion

A couple should only consider having children after their relationship has lasted a substantial time, preferably a few years. Then whether or not to have children should be decided on the basis of advice from friends, relatives and perhaps professional counselors.

Then, of course, the couple should make sure that their home is suitable for children and that their finances are sufficient and secure for the long term.

Finally, they should try to imagine whether a child would want to live in their home with them, or would it prefer other, better circumstances.

Most important of all, the relationship should be a permanent one because parents are the most important influence in a child's life.

As Morgan et al. (1979) put it:

For many reasons, the family is the prime site for observational learning during childhood. Parents are children's first models as well as their first teachers. They are also very powerful figures in young children's lives, controlling all resources and caring for all needs. Children watch their parents do many things which look like fun, and see that many skills their parents have are effective (lead to better reinforcement) than their own skills.

Thus to give children a good start in life a stable, adequately financed and happy marriage is required.

Then both parents should stick at the task of keeping family life happy and secure and make a considerable effort at teaching and bringing up their children as best they can.

Chapter 19

MAKING MARRIAGE WORK

*To be required to sleep with the same woman forever was a
curious and unnatural idea to him, to be expected to dredge up
enthusiasm for old acts, and routine plays,
he wondered at the arrogance of the female.*
Tom Morrison, *The Bluest Eye* (1970).

*I did not sleep. I never do when I am over-happy,
under-happy, or in bed with a strange man.*
Edna O'Brien, *The Love Object* (1968).

Mohr's Law of Politics

Making marriage, or an equivalent relationship, work is less than easy. Mohr's Law of Politics is that build a 'fence' of any kind and there will be people in substantial numbers on either side of it as potential competitors (Mohr, 2018b).

Some political divisions are comparatively arbitrary compared to the considerable differences between men and women, some of which were discussed in earlier chapters of this book.

Women's ability to bear children is a very major difference, one that men are somewhat in awe of. Women, on the other hand, are sometimes in awe of men's greater strength and, indeed, sometimes in fear of it. The latter difference we evolved with and it was the basis of our survival in our troglodyte hunter-gathering days.

As noted in Chapter 21 there are many other differences between two marriage partners. As Baker (2004) points out:

Gender aside, the potential for conflicts continues to abound. We come from difference places and are affected more than we understand by our family of origin.

Then, for example only, there are differences in personality, habitual behavioural differences, differences in educational and work background, and differences in likes and dislikes.

Communication

Lack of effective and constructive communication is the great problem of the human race. What makes us unique amongst animals is our enlarged cerebral cortex that stores the semantic memory required for our advanced languages.

Yet throughout history we have continued to behave just like the chimps that Jane Goodall (van Lawick-Goodall, 1971) was so disillusioned by, we have periodic conflicts with other groups of people, be it tribes, nations or followers of another religion.

This is largely because of a lack of *effective* communication and thence *understanding* of other people.

Such understanding is, of course, made more difficult when people speak a different language, but men and women also, in effect, speak different languages to some extent at least, in part because of their different upbringing, and thence different issues and related vocabulary, as discussed in Chapter 7.

As a result of their different, somewhat socially stereotyped, upbringing, men and women have different values. Women, of course, care more about children, in part owing to the powerful maternal instinct discussed in Chapter 6. Men, on the other hand, care more about the football team they follow winning, and such comparatively trivial pursuits tend to alienate them from many women.

There are many more minor differences. Women care much more about their appearance, having been brought up supposed to look beautiful. Men's business suits, on the other hand, relate to army uniforms and are designed to make them look stupid, not hard to do.

These differences, of course, make communication difficult. As a somewhat tongue-in-cheek test of this, try sending a member of an all-male board to a meeting dressed as a woman!

In a marital-type relationship, however, I would recommend that the partners have some sort of discussion every day or two. At this they can air their respective gripes about each other, if any, and it is far better to bring them out in the open in this way than risk the other partner complaining to other people about you as this may result in rumours which may be damaging to your reputation.

Perhaps more important, the partners should discuss any problems they may be having at work as these may pose a risk to a partner's career. Problems with their children should, of course, also be discussed.

Finally, financial matters should be discussed occasionally to make sure that the family financial situation is sound.

Partnership

A marital-type relationship should, of course, be a partnership and the work should be shared. In the traditional male breadwinner scenario housewives would always complain that they were still busy cooking and dealing with children after the man had finished work, giving rise to the old saying: "A woman's work is never done."

Today, a high proportion of wives are also employed at least part-time, as noted in Chapter 22, often requiring expensive day care for children, and this places a considerable financial stress on many families that are also struggling to pay substantial rents or mortgages.

Even when both partners work full-time, however, most women find themselves doing most of the housework, leading to continuing complaints:

Women still do around 80 per cent of home chores and caring tasks, despite their increased workforce participation. Helene Couprie, Time Allocation within the Family, Economic Journal, 2007.

It found single working women spent an average of ten hours a week doing housework and single men seven hours. After becoming a couple, women's housework time shot up to 15 hours a week, while the average male contribution dropped to five hours, even when both spouses work outside the home (Caro & Fox, 2008).

The problem relates to the traditional housewife role of women, of course, and the solution is that men should be encouraged to spend more time helping with both housework and caring for and teaching children.

If the working woman cum housewife then has a little more spare time that can be spent relaxing and talking with their partner, thus helping keep the relationship working congenially and effectively.

Healthy life

Healthy lifestyle should be a primary objective in every family, this including sound diet, watching one's weight, getting enough exercise, getting plenty of quality sleep, and getting enough relaxation time.

A healthy diet should, of course, include plenty of vegetables and a little fruit, limit fat (particularly saturated and trans fat) and thence meat (especially red meat), limit fatty fast food, limit fatty and salty snack foods, and limit sugary confectionary and drinks.

Children should limit sugar, of course, to protect their teeth, also brushing them soon after eating. Indeed, I find it lamentable that there is no provision for this at school.

Watching one's weight and exercise, of course, go together, and it is important to keep one's weight fairly close to that recommended for one's height and sex (Mohr, 2012b, 2013, 2015, 2018c).

To help build strong bodies children should have about an hour of exercise daily, including walking, and when old enough they should be encouraged to do an average of half an hour of more strenuous exercise daily.

For good health the same exercise requirements apply to adults, regular medium intensity exercise being required for a healthy heart and circulation system, for example.

A few hours of relaxation time is also necessary and this, of course, can include such entertainments as TV, music and reading.

For adults circa 8 hours of good quality sleep is necessary for good mental and physical health. Here the shared double bed can be a problem. If, for example, one partner snores, as is often the case, that can pose serious problems. Lonely young children invading the room in the middle of the night is another problem lessened (roughly halved, in fact) if the parents have separate rooms.

Sexual intercourse is merely an act of breeding which humans, being in most respects the most stupid creatures on the planet, as our always troubled history suggests, attach much too much importance to. As I like to say, sex was God's joke on mankind and we are too stupid to see it.

On the issue of satisfactory sex, according to the landmark Kinsey report, 10 percent of married women had never had orgasm during sexual intercourse, and 25 percent had not had orgasm during the first year of marriage (Lindzey et al, 1978).

I think that a couple's sex life might be better if they slept in separate beds, if not separate rooms, especially if one partner snores. Then, refreshed by sleeping well each night, a little 'mucking around' could be done on a more occasional basis if both partners had a double bed, even if in separate rooms, but perhaps with a shared bathroom between them.

The bottom line is that sharing a bed for life with the same ultimately rotting thing is arguably insane, and certainly physically unhealthy, if not distasteful, if one had half one's wits left that is.

Conclusion

One problem in marriage is that, as noted in Chapters 2 and 3, young men are not brought up thinking about children and romance. Often they are really just finding their way in the world a little when they have their first sexual relationship or two with women. When they all too often end up with unplanned for children they are completely unprepared for the situation.

Young women, on the other hand, have been brought up playing with dolls, and for them children are a raison d'etre. In addition, they see getting married to some nice man and having children as being romantic. Indeed, much of the huge publishing and movie industries are based on this.

Thus, when the somewhat humdrum reality of marriage with wailing children emerges women are often quite disillusioned.

No doubt that is why we call that holiday taken after marriage the honeymoon, because reality will hit when the honeymoon ends, of course.

For marriage to work the relationship must have been a carefully chosen one in the beginning, as discussed in Chapter 21. Then the marriage should only have been made after careful thought and advice, and after the relationship has endured for a substantial amount of time.

More important still, children should only be had if the relationship is likely to last, and after plenty of thought, discussion, advice and counseling, along with proper career and financial planning.

Then, to keep the partnership working well, frequent and effective communication and planning is required, along with optimism or 'hope' (GA, RS & PE Mohr., 2018b), to ensure a healthy and happy life for the whole family.

Chapter 20

MAKING YOUR CHILDREN SMARTER

In the present writer's survey of Army recruits (Vernon, 1951), for example, the average I.Q. of those who were only children, or who had but one sibling, was about 106; but with each additional child sibling the figure declined till those from families of 13 and over averaged only 87.
Philip Vernon, *Intelligence and Attainment Tests* (1960).

Introduction

As noted in the quotation above, having only one or two children makes them more likely to have a higher IQ, doubtless because of the greater resources and attention able to be given to the children.

Indeed, China's one child policy of the last couple of decades may be further proof of this because average intelligence in that part of Asia is now, at circa 100.25, slightly above that for the UK and USA (supposedly about 100, but I suspect somewhat less [Mohr, 2012a; Mohr & Fear, 2016; Mohr et al., 2018a]).

Man's population is also at least double what is sustainable with any degree of comfort (Mohr, 2012a), so having only one or two children is the only sensible course on that score.

As noted in earlier chapters, care should always be taken in family planning, waiting until financial and emotional stability of the relationship is assured before having children.

It should also be noted that, as Lynn and Vanhaven (2002) point out, we have dysgenic fertility trends so that the least intelligent people have the most children.

Carlo Cipolla (1974) pointed out that our population growth graph went almost vertical with the coming of the industrial revolution and implored that what we needed was 'quality not quantity,' a phrase I recall my fifth grade teacher Miss Bachelard repeating often.

As noted in earlier chapters, in seeking a compatible partner intelligence is a key criterion. Then couples with higher intelligence might expect at least equally intelligent children, the desirable outcome.

Couples should also be aware of epigenic marking before having children because traits such as obesity are passed on in that way. Thus it is also possible that traits such as exercising or thinking a lot might be passed on also.

Early brain development

At birth the human brain is relatively large compared to the body. Almost all the neural cells that will ever be available are present but only a basic network of the *axons* and *dendrites* that connect *neurons* together exists. Further connections develop as the infant learns basic perception and motor skills, the long *axons* that extend from the brain cells then receiving signals from *receptor cells,* such as the small hair cells in the inner ear, or sending signals to *effector cells* in the muscles.

This development in the bulk of the brain parallels that in all animal species and is that necessary for basic functioning and survival. What sets humans apart is the considerable development of the *cerebral cortex*, the envelope of brain cells that covers the brain, and where our thinking and storage of abstract memory information such as language occurs.

Development of the articulatory mechanisms required for controlled speech and the cortical mechanisms that control them is a slow maturational process that occurs in *Broca's area* of the frontal cortex. It has been suggested that babbling, however, is a sub cortical process.

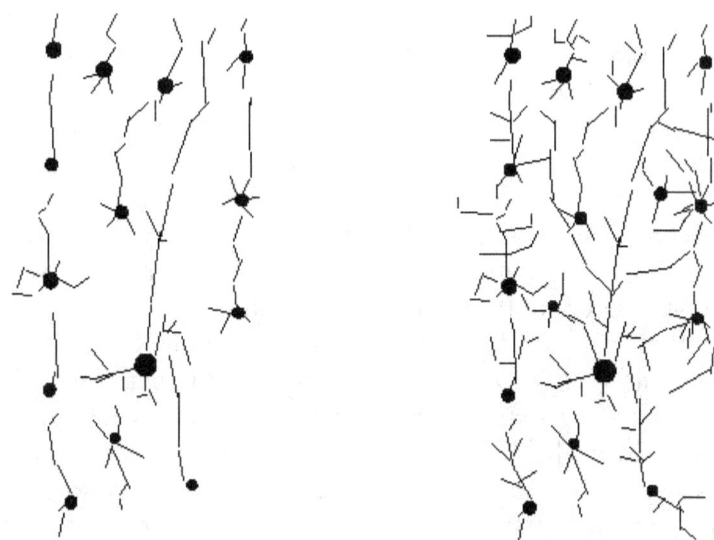

Figure 20.1. Postnatal development of the human cerebral cortex around Broca's Area (language related):
(a) newborn; (b) 1 month.

Semantic memory of language is stored in *Wernicke's area* of the temporal lobe of the cerebral cortex.

Figure 20.1(a) shows a small part of the cerebral cortex of a newborn child in which long *axons* extend from the neurons and form branches. Fine *terminal arbors* at the end of these branches connect at *synapses* to the short *dendrites* surrounding other neurons. Figure 20.1(b) shows considerably more dendrites and branching of the axons at the age of one month (Foss & Hakes, 1978). At the age of 24 months the neural network is a good deal denser.

At birth every neuron can connect with 2,500 other neurons. At age 2 or 3 there are 2 billion neurons and each can connect to up to 15,000 other neurons (Holford, 2008). The network continues to develop in following years and the neurons, while not increasing in number, do increase in size.

In addition, the motor nerve pathways that control such activities as speech production must gradually develop sheaths of the protein *myelin* that prevent 'short-circuiting' of impulses between nerve tracts.

As a result of this gradual brain development each human characteristic is developed at a different rate.

Eye coordination, for example, develops much more rapidly than speech. Nevertheless, for the first few months the infant may smile at any moving object such as a dummy head whereas later it may be upset by the faces of strangers.

Packard (1978) cites a vivid example of the importance of timing. In this two Harvard researchers studied the way kittens learnt to recognize shapes and patterns, a physiological ability that develops in the fourth week. If the kittens were blindfolded for this week they effectively became blind for life. There appear, therefore, to be periods when the infant's brain is extraordinarily receptive to behavioural and personality development so that it is easiest to change a child's intelligence for better or worse before the age of four.

Vocabulary growth in early childhood

When children reach the age of one the pace at which learning can take place greatly increases.

Now learning can be accomplished with a host of aids such as pictures, simple books and educational toys.

By this formative age the child has been out and about a good deal and optimistic attempts have been made to teach it many words of which it will have learnt only a few.

As shown in Table 20.1, however, word learning occurs at a quite rapid rate from here on, to the point at which a basic command of language has been obtained at age five.

Table 20.1. Words learnt with age.

Age (years)	Words learnt
1	3-5
1.25	15
1.5	25
1.75	100
2	250
2.5	450
3	900
4	1550
4.5	1900
5	2100
5.5	2300
6	2550

Whilst the first year is instrumental in learning to begin to talk, in the second year a comparatively massive growth in vocabulary occurs. Thereafter the rate of increase is approximately linear but slows down as the child comes to grip with a widening range of subjects at school.

Note that care should be taken to teach children numbers amongst their earliest words, and to teach them to make simple sums such as $2 + 2 = 4$.

By the time they have learnt to read a little, however, children are able to learn things by *cognitive* learning which *processes* and stores *abstract* information.

At this stage they can be taught concepts such as good and bad, and this is in turn helpful in motivating their learning progress.

Finally, one should aim for a child being at least a little ahead of the results of Table 20.1, and having comparable performance in numeracy to that of Table 20.1.

The early learning centre

At the outset an infant's cot and simple learning objects that might be placed in view of it are the child's first learning centre. When a child is about one year old this learning centre might be upgraded to a small child's table plus simple books and other educational aids and toys.

The importance of this *enrichment* of the child's learning environment was tellingly demonstrated by the work of social psychologist David Krech and his group at UC Berkeley (Packard, 1978).

In this they provided a group of rats with an "enriched environment" of large cages with various things rats enjoy such as slides, wheels and the like. Then a maze with a sugar reward at the end was added. This had a dark and a lighted alley and the rats soon learnt which led to the sugar. Then the maze lighting was reversed regularly so that the rats had to relearn the 'sugar route.'

A second control group of rats lived normally and a third group was kept in a deprived dark and noiseless area.

After 90 days it was found that the 'enriched' rats had developed thicker cerebral cortexes!

This was perhaps the first evidence that the brain is modified by experience. The enrichment conditions caused the following changes (Atrens & Curthoys, 1982):

[1] The size of the cerebral cortex was increased.
[2] The size of the cortical neurons increased.
[3] The size and number of synaptic contacts increased.
[4] The quantity of acetylcholinesterase, the compound responsible for breakdown of the neurotransmitter acetylcholine, increased.

Therefore, the rats which had experienced early environmental enrichment were apparently anatomically and biochemically superior to those which had endured a deprived environment.

This result provided laboratory evidence that environmental enrichment might be able to reverse the deficiencies in brain development resulting from an environmentally deprived childhood.

The conclusion, of course, is that, just as physical exercise is good for your body, mental exercise helps develop the brain, perhaps in synergy with an enriched physical environment that includes physical activities involving some intelligence and skill.

Maria Montessori provided evidence that an enriched environment accelerates human learning ability by taking poor children in Rome and placing them in stimulating classrooms with many interesting puzzles and objects to work with. The children were reading enthusiastically by three or four and were well into geometry by five or six.

If follows that the investment of a modest amount of money in setting up and equipping a child's personal learning centre might be a wise one.

Increasingly the child will have learnt to spend time in this engaged in learning activities such as looking at picture books, drawing, learning to write, and so on.

Parents should also have made a point of not only supervising this important activity at least intermittently but also joining in for a substantial session of one-on-one instruction.

By now the child is capable of discussing its problems and progress and asking questions that might help solve problems and assist progress. Therefore, the parent should make a point of allowing a time period of at least several minutes every few days in which to talk with the child in this way.

The importance of the home environment was emphasized in a study by Bradley and Caldwell (1967) in which an inventory of favourable factors in the home was compared to the results from a test of the infant's development:

A group of 77 normal children was given an infant development test and a home assessment inventory at age 6 months, and the Stanford-Binet at age 3 years.

*It was found that the home inventory
predicted IQ at age 3 better than did
the infants' own mental development at 6 months!
Children with increasing scores had mothers who were involved
with them and provided appropriate play materials;
those with decreasing scores tended to live in homes
where material things and daily events were disorganized.*

Much of the correlation between home environment and IQ development can be ascribed to heredity but a study by Skodal and Skeels (1949) showed that improved environment increased children's IQs by an average of 20 points above that of their mothers.

Two heads are better than one

It is, of course, better when both parents take an active part in a child's home learning. Having two teachers 'on the same page' about everything taught will, of course, reinforce the child's learning efforts.

In addition, variation from a woman's softer touch to a man's perhaps more goal-oriented approach can help with progression through longer learning tasks.

It has been found that correlation of intelligence with parent's occupation is slightly less than that for genes (Vernon, 1960), there being, of course, a correlation between occupations and intelligence in any case.

More important, regardless of a parent's occupation, if one of their roles is active teaching of the child that may have a far more important bearing on the child's IQ development than the parent's occupation outside the home.

A sound routine for home learning should be established, perhaps involving a combination of day care or learning groups (as discussed in the next section) and home sessions once or twice a day and of duration ranging from half an hour to an hour, depending on the child's age.

Small learning groups

Packard (1978) raised the interesting possibility of the use of professional people to teach by modeling.

These people would be trained to know the periods during which learning of various areas of knowledge can best be commenced, and in how best to use modeling techniques to initiate that learning. Such people would then visit the home or attend play group sessions.

Packard noted that an experiment with a form of group modeling was undertaken at New York Medical College. This began with twenty pairs of mothers and babies when the babies were only four weeks old and lasted three years at the end of which the children were compared with those of a control group.

The children in the experimental group were a good deal more advanced in language and other skills than the control group.

Indeed, some experts doubt the competence of the modern family for child rearing and believe that more professional efforts are essential to help develop emotional stability and intellectual development in infants.

As an example of this, Weiss and Mann (1978) refer to a project in Milwaukee that found that children given more attention by the mother or a specially trained teacher, showed markedly higher IQ.

Enhancing the learning process

The home learning process can be enhanced by such means as the 'Superlearning' recommended by Ostrander and Schroeder (1979). This involves encouraging physical and psychological relaxation with quite background music, slow breathing exercises, and visualizing nice scenes to achieve a reflective and receptive frame of mind.

Then the child is encouraged to affirm: "I can do it."

Here, developing a positive attitude is comparable to the 'teacher expectancy effect' where it is found that students who already get good marks are encouraged to do even better by a combination of the positive results, the confidence they obtain from these, and the 'expectation' and confidence the teacher shows about their ability.

With the scene set, the parent/teacher reads the material aloud at a careful pace while the child reads it silently. This is repeated again with quiet background music and the child is then tested on the material.

Home schooling

In the USA home schooling has increased markedly in recent decades. The number of home-schooled children grew from just a few thousand in the early 1970s to 1.1 million in 2003, having increased 30% between 1999 and 2003 (Penn, 2007).

In 2000, only 52 percent of colleges had formal admission policies for home-schooled students, but by 2005 85% did, in that year a study showing that home-schooled students scored 81 points higher than the national average on the SAT (Penn, 2007).

Though home-schooled children were only 2% of school-age children, they were 12% of the students in the National Spelling Bee and in three out of seven years a home-schooled child won the National Geography Bee (Penn, 2007).

In 2001, a home-schooled boy from Montana completed high school at 15. Not feeling ready for college, he wrote the novel *Eragon* which become a best-seller and was released as a movie in 2006 (Penn, 2007).

Certainly, therefore, children taught well at both home and school should do better!

The first author remembers a little rainy Sunday afternoon home instruction and thus, for example, being able to count to 100 at age 4. By age 9 and in grade 4 he was equal top of the class in arithmetic and did fairly well thereafter, finishing school and his first degree with first class honours.

He also remembers going to an expensive private school where there was far too much emphasis on extra-curricular activities, in part to impress upon the parents that they were getting their money's worth, but that he would have preferred more freedom to develop his own lifestyle.

In addition, as always at school, if not University, there is total reliance on rote learning of standard academic material, and little or no instruction on life skills, for example how to deal with such issues as sex, bullying, smoking, and booze (to which list one would now add drugs, of course).

Teenagers should also be taught how to decide as soon as possible upon a realistically achievable career goal and advised on how to achieve it. They should also be instructed how to survive in the workplace, for example how to deal with bullying workmates or bosses.

IQ building

Measurable intelligence or IQ becomes meaningful by the age of four so that before that some effort should be made to 'build IQ' to give the child a head start.

The subject of IQ is sometimes controversial, particularly concerning differences in racial intelligence, but most experts consider that socioeconomic and cultural disadvantages are the main cause of any such differences.

Opinions also differ on what IQ tests really measure, some believing that they simply provide a measure of prior education. Binet, however, originally devised his classical test to measure the causes of learning retardation in public school pupils with a view to providing special classes for slow learners.

To help ensure that young children get a head start some conscious attempt should be made to 'build' their IQ at the age of three, if not before.

Most parents are well meaning and, at the outset at least, many imagine what prodigies their children perhaps are.

The very same parents, however, are those most likely to spoil the child with generosity and he or she may become a stubborn child and a less than good learner because of it.

It is for that reason that input from other parents, for example in play groups, and from professionals, for example in kindergartens, is important.

As for building IQ, the first believes one obvious step that can be taken is to note the questions in typical IQ tests, for example the Weschler Preschool and Primary Scale of Intelligence (WPPSI), example questions for which can easily be found on the Internet.

Then care can be taken to ensure that the child is taught the simple object identification and number and word recognition exercises it should be capable of at age three.

In case I am thought a hard task master in talking of IQ tests with 3-year-olds, here are a few examples of questions from Binet's intelligence test:

How old are you?
What are the names of these four colours?
Hand me five blocks from that pile.
What is the opposite of the word large?
Which one of these objects is different from the rest?
Point to your nose?

Figure 20.2 shows an example Weschler Preschool and Primary Scale of Intelligence question.

These are none too hard and the point is that a teacher can devise their own test and, as Binet set as a criterion, if on average students in the class can answer 75% of the questions, the test is representative of the norm for that age group, locally at least.

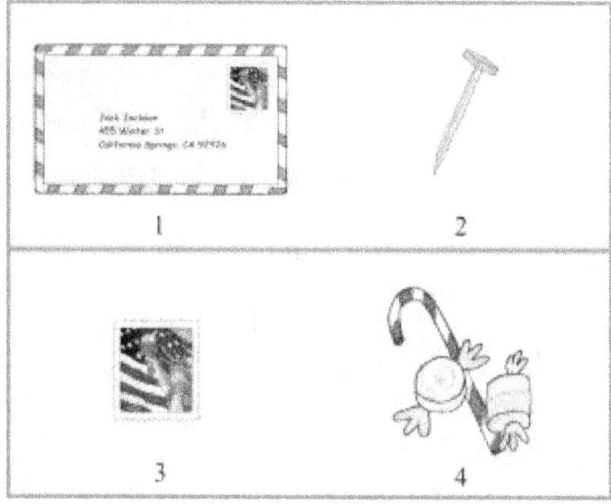

Figure 20.2. Pre-K to Kindergarten WPPSI question:
Which two pictures show the same thing?
{I have improved/simplified the original question. GAM]

As Weiss and Mann (1978) put it: *A person's (or a population's) IQ measures the ability to take IQ tests; it does not measure intelligence.*

Be that as it may, IQ tests do provide some measurement of level of learning and it is vitally important to ensure that the young child does not start school at a disadvantage.

Whether they measure learning or intelligence, or perhaps both, IQ test results generally correspond fairly well with the academic performance of children at school.

Note too that separate IQ tests are available for verbal, spatial, and numerical ability and these tell more about an individual than just a single IQ score.

Therefore, any small learning difficulty identified by an early IQ test can probably be remedied quickly, avoiding much greater difficulties further down the educational track.

In addition, such tests provide an opportunity to observe other aspects of performance such as motivation, persistence or maladaptive behaviours.

Remember also the vivid example given earlier in the chapter of Krech's rats with an enriched environment being found to have developed larger cerebral cortexes, a result which strongly supports Weiss and Mann's view (1978):

Even if we assume that IQ tests measure something like intelligence, we have to recognize that, like many other variable traits, intelligence is very much influenced by the environment.

There is a strong incentive, therefore, for parents to ensure that a child has at least a modestly endowed personal learning centre.

When there is more than one child in the family, of course, sharing of educational resources and experiences should be encouraged, especially when the children are of similar ages.

Nutritional supplements to improve IQ

Dr A.C. Kubala et. al. divided 351 students into two groups, those with higher, and those with lower vitamin C levels. Those with higher C levels were 4.5 points higher in IQ (Holford, 2009).

In another study, Patrick Holford, Stephen Schoenhaler, John Yudkin, Hans Eysenck and Linus Pauling gave 30 children a special multivitamin and mineral supplement and 30 others a placebo. After 8 months the supplement children's average non-verbal IQ[3] was 10 points higher, with some children being up to 20 points higher. Several other studies have had similar findings.

Another study of 200 teenagers in Dakota found that 20 mg (but not 10mg, the RDI being 7 mg) of zinc increased memory accuracy and attention spans (Holford & Colson, 2008).

---

[3] Non-verbal IQ is more fluid and susceptible to brain chemistry, while verbal IQ is more influenced by teaching.

Contrastingly, MIT researchers found that children with diets high in refined carbohydrates such as sugar, white bread and sweets, had IQ up to 25 points lower (Schauss, 1983).

Some of the studies that have made such findings have sometimes included infants, improved IQ from diet improvements showing up a few years down the track. Thus, pregnant women would be wise to ensure that their diets are as healthy as possible and include key nutrients such as the omega essential oils, B-complex, C, and zinc (Holford & Colson, 2008).

Conclusion

Children's brains develop most rapidly in the earliest years and maximum advantage should be taken of this by teaching them as much as possible at home.

To that end a child should have a personal learning centre reflective of the Montessori tradition and both parents should take part in routine educational sessions.

In these it is best to encourage and teach a child to rise above the expected level of learning for their age by, for example, teaching them simple addition at an early age.

In addition, it is best to have the child join learning groups at least occasionally, perhaps run by an educator trained for the purpose. Failing that, friends and neighbours with children of the same age group can be found to help run regular 'play and learn' sessions.

Children will also do better if one has "a nurturing and accepting family system" with plenty of encouragement, tolerance etc. (McGraw, 2004).

Finally, note that sound diet and appropriate supplementation can also help increase IQ.

PART V
SOCIAL LIFE

Chapter 21

SOCIAL ACTIVITIES

*A successful social technique consists perhaps in finding
unobjectionable means for individual self-assertion.*
Eric Hoffer, *The Passionate State of Mind* (1955).

Social support

Social life is generally considered important, solitude being associated with loneliness, depression etc.

More important, perhaps, is that when things go wrong it is helpful to have supportive people, whether they be relatives, friends, or counselors, to turn to for advice and moral support.

Such people can provide help and encouragement that may provide hope in the most difficult of circumstances, and hope alone in most cases will help one cope in the short term.

Then, in the longer term, one can begin to fix the problem(s) in question, or 'move on' from them to work towards new goals.

Successful businesswoman Lillian Vernon recalls: *My father told me I had talent and a good idea for starting a business and I should never let anything get in the way of fulfilling my dream, or I would regret it for the rest of my life,* concluding: *So don't let challenges, setbacks, or detractors defeat or discourage you. If you believe in yourself and think positively, you will succeed* (Trump, 2004).

There are many activities, hobbies etc. via which one can meet and socialize with people, some of these being briefly discussed in the following chapter.

Sporting clubs and associations

An Australia, Australian Rules Football (AFL) is very popular, membership of some Australian Football League clubs totaling circa 100,000 members (for Collingwood it is 180,00 members), attendances at many games often being circa 90,000.

In Eastern states Rugby is also very popular, having two 'codes', the Australian Rugby Union, and the Australian Rugby League. Attendances for ARU and ARL games are typically 20,000 to 30,000.

In several countries cricket is a major sport, the "Ashes" tests series between Australia and England, and the Indian Premier League being of particular note, and having large attendances of up to 100,000.

Tennis remains a very popular sport globally, as evidenced by large attendances at the four "Grand Slam" tournaments in England, France, the USA, and Australia, and there are tennis venues and clubs in almost every suburb and town of substantial size in Australia.

Lawn bowls is also popular in many countries, Australia having lawn bowls clubs in most major suburbs of large cities with substantial memberships, mostly retired and elderly people.

Golf remains popular in many Western countries, the many suburban golf courses in Australia having substantial memberships and large clubhouses for social activities.

Horse racing is also a major sport in several countries, also providing an opportunity for plenty of socializing between races, as well as afterwards.

Several other sports also provide opportunities for socializing, including trotting (horses), greyhound racing, surfing, shooting, gyms, basketball, and netball.

Social clubs

There are many clubs formed for purely social purposes, examples in Melbourne, Australia, including the somewhat exclusive Melbourne and the Atheneum club.

Clubs and pubs

Pubs have a long history of providing social contacts between 'regulars', and an opportunity to meet people and make new friends.

In Australia there are now there are many "clubs" with dozens of poker machines which provide most of their revenue, with old-fashioned pubs with only a bar now regularly closing down.

These clubs also have bars and restaurants, and often have organized social groups which meet regularly.

Nightclubs and dances

In the central suburbs of major cities nightclubs provide late night booze and an opportunity socialize, and in particular meet and dance with members of the opposite sex.

There are also regular weekend dances organized at council-owned premises, most of these attended by young people with, or looking for, a girl or boy friend.

Writers groups

In many major cities many major cities there are several writers groups where people who have writing as a hobby meet once a month, some groups publishing a book of collected works by members every year.

Some members of such groups do write a book or two, sometimes using the growing 'self-publishing' industry to publish their books, and occasionally succeeding in find 'traditional' publisher to print and market their books.

These writers groups, however, are largely a social exercise providing an opportunity to meet like-minded people.

Art clubs

Few in number, there are a few arts clubs in which both amateur and professional artists meets and socialize and share ideas.

Religious activities

Religious services, of course, provide a regular opportunity to meet people afterwards, some churches, for example having a community lunch after their weekly Sunday service.

Most churches, synagogues etc. have a committee which meets regularly, sometimes organizing occasional social evenings for members of the congregation.

The use of 'confessionals' by the Catholic Church is worth note, but the authors believe it would be more helpful if churches provided a 'complaints service' instead in which people could air their problems. Not far from where the first author lives, however, the Anglican Church runs a community consultation service where people can discuss life problems.

Conclusion

There are many activities, clubs, and other organizations that provide an opportunity for social contact.

Many of these organizations have regular meetings, sometimes purely for social purposes.

Branch meetings of political parties are of particular note, and meetings and politics are discussed in the following chapter.

Chapter 22

MEETINGS

*No grand idea was ever born in a conference, but a lot of
foolish ideas have died there.*
F. Scott Fitzgerald, *The Crack-Up*, "Notebook E" (1945).

*Politics is supposed to be the second oldest profession. I have come to
realize that it bears a very close resemblance to the first.*
Ronald Reagan, at a conference in Los Angeles, 2 March 1977.

Formal meetings

In business, as in politics, meetings are an important part of
the process. As in parliament, standard procedures should be
followed in calling, running and reporting meetings.

To publicize an impending meeting an agenda paper is
distributed, for example (Renton, 1972):

BULLDUST ASSOCIATION OF VICTORIA

Annual General Meeting to be held at 1, Spring St at 8:00
p.m. on Friday 14/9/2018.
BUSINESS
1. Chairperson's opening remarks.
2. Apologies.
3. Minutes of the AGM held on 10/8/2018.
4. Business arising out of the minutes.
5. Correspondence.
6. Business arising out of the correspondence.
7. President's report (AGM only).
8. Treasurer's report.

9. Election of new members.
10. Subcommittee reports/Reports from delegates.
11. Election of office bearers:
President, Vice-president(s) (1 or 2), Chairperson, Secretary, Treasurer,
Committee (circa 5)
12. Election of auditor.
13. Guest speaker: Mr. J.C. Smith, former Prime Minister, on "Politics Today."
14. Motions on notice:
a. Mr. Jones to move, "That the secretary be granted an honorarium of ten dollars ($10)."
b. Mrs. Brown to move, "That the Government be requested to reduce the sales tax on bull dust."
15. General business.
16. Notice of motions.
17. Date of next meeting.
18. Close.

During such a meeting the secretary will keep notes and these are used to prepare the *minutes* of the meeting, copies of which are sent to members and other interested parties prior to the next meeting.

These should cover such items as:

Present
Apologies
1. Minutes of previous meeting
2. Financial report
3. Issue A: report on discussion, suggestions, resolutions etc.
4. Issue B: report on etc.
5. General business, discussion etc.
6. Next meeting: date/time.
"The meeting then closed."
Signed . . . ., Chairperson &/or President.

In the matter of meetings of businesses and associations the following additional subjects are worth consideration:

Chairperson. The chairperson's duties are simply to ensure that the agenda is followed and to deal with motions.

Motions. A motion is a proposed *resolution*. It may be:
a. Procedural, for example "That the meeting adjourn."
b. Substantive, for example "That ABC's account be paid."
A motion is dealt with as follows:
<u>Mover:</u> states (preferably in writing) the motion and explains it.
<u>Seconder:</u> (called by the chairperson) speaks for the motion.
<u>Speaker(s):</u> alternatively speak against/for the motion.
<u>Mover:</u> summarizes the case for the motion.
<u>Chairperson:</u>
"The motion is that - - -."
"The question is that the motion be agreed to."
"Those in favour?"
"Those against?"
"I declare the motion carried/lost."
Note that motions can be:
1. In parts (a), (b) etc.
2. Amended.
3. Rescinded.
4. Foreshadowed.

Procedural motions. These generally have two functions:
a. To dispose of business, for example "That the meeting adjourn" or "That the speaker be no longer heard."
b. To deal with business, for example to vary the order of business or to call for a vote ("That the motion be put").

"Point of order". This exclamation to the Chairperson is a complaint, for example, that the speaker has taken too long, is out of order (poor language) or is not speaking on the subject.
Voting methods: These include
(1) Voices/show of hands.
(2) Division.
(3) Poll or ballot (which may be secret).

Constitutions: Associations, companies etc. should have a constitution that contains usually standard clauses governing behaviour of the company and its members, the running of meetings and other matters requiring rules. Some of the most common clauses are:

Name, objectives, membership and subscription clauses.

Meetings, committee, elections and quorum clauses.

Finance, dissolution, voting and amendments clauses.

Interpretations, delegations, open/closed meetings and expulsion clauses.

Standing orders: These are the rules for the procedure of meetings, for example setting time limits for meetings and stating the procedure for putting motions.

Election systems: Prior to an election such matters as the following should be considered:

1. A call for nominations.
2. Provision for postal or proxy votes.
3. Appointment of a returning officer.
4. Method of election, for example:
a. First past the post, or
b. Preferential/proportional/points systems.

On matters such election systems the reader may require a little further reading to learn more detail but, generally, so far as meetings are concerned, it is also a good idea to attend one or two properly run ones.

There are also a few rare books on procedure for meetings. The first author remembers buying one over 50 years ago (Renton, 1972) and taking great delight in moving at a University board meeting:

"That the speaker be no longer heard until he can speak to the meeting properly prepared" (the chap kept fumbling through pages of his proposal and changing his mind when asked any question).

I am sure they had never heard of such a motion. Anyway it was carried and the offender gave me dirty looks around the institution for weeks afterwards.

Political meetings

Politics, of course, is very much about meetings, ranging from local branch meetings to the farcical 'raving clown show' of the antiquated and Westminster Parliamentary system of two major opposing parties yelling at each other from opposite sides of the "chamber".

The problems of this outdated system, of course, is that after a period or two of government by 'Party A', the two major parties swap places and much of the legislation of the preceding few years is undone now that 'Party B' is in government.

In this situation Mohr's Law of Politics prevails, that is, build a 'fence' of any kind and there will be people in substantial numbers on either side of it as potential competitors (Mohr, 2012a; Mohr et al., 2018b). Note that, with this law in mind, it is sometimes wise not to tell some people, particularly those in one's workplace, which political party one supports.

To overcome this 'revolving door' farce of the 2-party Westminster system, the first author proposes that we should have 'Real democracy' in which there would be no 'parties' as such, but candidates in each electorate would stand as independents, and the leader of the country would be elected and confirmed by a regular parliamentary vote.

Membership of the local branch of a political party, however, does provide a good deal of social contact with plenty of opportunity for discussion and sharing of views and opinions.

Helping in election campaigns, for example by 'door knocking', or handing out flyers at shopping centres and on election day, also provides opportunities to meet people and perhaps make a few new friends.

Regular local government council meetings can also be attended, perhaps providing an opportunity to meet people and make new and useful contacts.

Group brainstorming

Meetings, however, are an important way of getting ideas and solving problems. In other words they are an important part of the human thinking process.

The practice of meetings for group brainstorming has been widely practiced with success and several factors have been found to improve results:

[1] People tend to have twice as many ideas in the group situation because of the more stimulating environment, 'cross fertilization' of ideas and arousal of competitive spirit.

[2] Scheduled alternation of individual and group thinking improves results.

[3] As more ideas are produced they tend to improve.

[4] Second sessions a few days later improve results because of 'incubation' etc.

[5] Screening of the results by a second group.

As discussed in earlier chapters 4 and 5, creative thinking to produce new ideas and solutions should be followed by critical thinking to evaluate them.

Conclusion

Meetings often provide a good opportunity to make new friends, perhaps with contacts that might prove useful when one needs help with an important life problem.

In addition, more formal meetings are good experience in relation to learning aspects of management, annual general meetings of company shareholders being a notable example.

There are many other types of meetings, of course, for example protest meetings about key social or local issues, and these too may provide an opportunity to find useful contacts and perhaps make new friends.

Chapter 23

NETWORKING

In companies whose wealth is intellectual capital, networks, rather than hierarchies, are the right organizational design.

Networks irrevocably subvert managerial authority.
Thomas A. Stewart, *Intellectual Capital* (1997).

Introduction

Having a 'network' of friends and contacts with whom one can share information and ideas, and from whom one might be able to get useful advice and help with life problems is, of course, important.

As discussed in the preceding two chapters, there are many ways in which one can meet people, ranging from sporting associations and groups to local branch meetings of political parties.

Now, of course, the Internet provides many opportunities for social contact by email or using such programs as Facebook and Twitter.

The following section gives a short BASIC program for determining the voltages at the 'nodes' of a Direct Current or DC network such as that used to illustrate the effects of hierarchy in an organization in Figure 14.1, the results illustrating just how much the power of the leader at the top increases as the size of the hierarchical network grows.

Then a further section gives Input-Output Analysis as an example of how companies interact financially, and such modeling can also be used for information exchanging.

DC network example

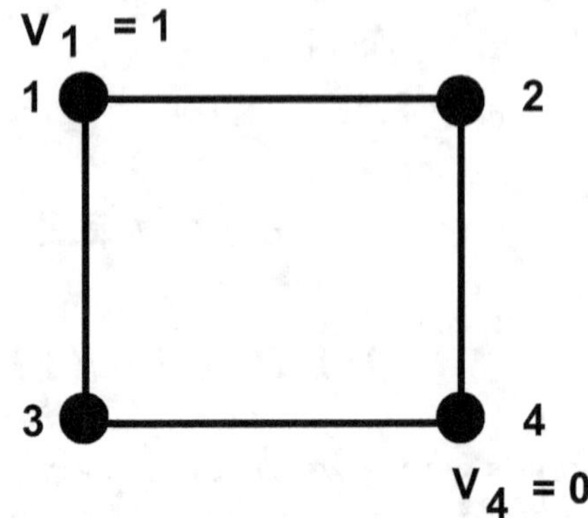

Figure 23.1. FEM model of simple DC network
Resistances 12, 13, 24, 34 all = 1.
Potential at node 1 is 1 and at node 4 it is 0.

As a simple example of network Figure 23.1 shows a direct current (DC) network with four resistance *elements* connecting four *nodes.* Here this will be modeled using the *Finite Element Method* (Mohr, 1992).

The numerical Finite Element model for this 'structure' is obtained by summing matrices for each element formed by using Ohm's Law to write the current flow in each element *ij* as

$$Q_{ij} = (V_i - V_j)/R_{ij}$$

where V_i and V_j are the voltages at nodes *i* and *j* at each end, and R_{ij} is the *resistance* of the element.

Then writing the two equations for current flow at each end of the element as a matrix we obtain the element equations

$$\left\{ \begin{array}{c} Q_{ij} \\ -Q_{ij} \end{array} \right\} = (1/R_{ij}) \left[\begin{array}{cc} 1 & -1 \\ -1 & 1 \end{array} \right] \left\{ \begin{array}{c} V_i \\ V_j \end{array} \right\} = k \left\{ \begin{array}{c} V_i \\ V_j \end{array} \right\}$$

Doing this for each element and writing the entries from their *element matrices k* into a *system matrix K* in positions corresponding to the node numbers for each element we obtain the system equations:

$$\{Q\} = \begin{Bmatrix} Q_1 \\ Q_2 \\ Q_3 \\ Q_4 \end{Bmatrix} = \begin{bmatrix} G_{12}+G_{13} & -G_{12} & -G_{13} & 0 \\ -G_{12} & G_{12}+G_{24} & 0 & -G_{24} \\ -G_{13} & 0 & G_{13}+G_{34} & -G_{34} \\ 0 & -G_{24} & -G_{34} & G_{24}+G_{34} \end{bmatrix} \begin{Bmatrix} V_1 \\ V_2 \\ V_3 \\ V_4 \end{Bmatrix} = K\{V\}$$

where $G_{12} = 1/R_{12}$ is the reciprocal of the resistance, or *conductance,* of element 12.

This *assembly* process for the system matrix is easily done by a computer program and the matrix problem can be solved using a short Gauss reduction routine (Mohr, 1992).

To 'load' the network either input or output currents must be specified at some nodes to 'force' current flows. Alternatively, differing voltages are specified for at least two nodes, one of these being a 'datum' potential equal to zero.

Here this is done in the program by calculating equivalent current 'loads' by multiplying the columns in the system matrix for 'specified voltage nodes' by the voltage specified at them and adding the result to the load matrix { Q } which is represented by array V( ) in the following program.

Then the problem is solved to determine the nodal voltages or potentials and the element currents are calculated using:

$$Q_{ij} = (V_i - V_j)/R_{ij}$$

A QBASIC short program that assembles and solves this problem is given below. Here key notation is

NN(,)	matrix storing the element node numbers
R( )	matrix storing the element resistances
C(,)	the system matrix
V( )	the nodal voltages
NP	number of nodes
NE	number of elements
NS	number of nodes with specified voltage
a$, b$	format specifier strings
X, S	temporary numbers

The program reads the data in lines 3, 5 and 9, 'deploying' the element matrices into the system matrix in lines 6 and 7 and modifying the RHS 'load' vector V( ) for the specified voltages in line 11. Then only lines 14 to 20 are required to solve the problem using Gauss reduction.

Here X is first used to store the *pivot* for 'row division' operations (line 14) and then used to store the 'row multiplier' (line 17) for the row subtraction operations (line 19) and doing these on the RHS vector V( ) (line 17) as well yields the solution.

Note that the RHS line numbers are for reference purposes only and are not part of the program and must be removed before it can be run.

```
DIM NN(20, 2), R(20), C(20, 20), V(20)                    1
a$ = "###": b$ = "######.###"                             2
READ NP, NE, NS                                           3
FOR K = 1 TO NE                                           4
READ I, J, R: NN(K, 1) = I: NN(K, 2) = J: R(K) = R        5
C(I, I) = C(I, I) + 1 / R: C(I, J) = C(I, J) - 1 / R      6
C(J, I) = C(J, I) - 1 / R: C(J, J) = C(J, J) + 1 / R      7
NEXT                                                      8
FOR K = 1 TO NS: READ N, S                                9
FOR I = 1 TO NP                                          10
C(N, I) = 0: V(I) = V(I) - S * C(I, N)                   11
C(I, N) = 0: NEXT I                                      12
V(N) = S: C(N, N) = 1: NEXT                              13
FOR I = 1 TO NP: X = C(I, I): V(I) = V(I) / X            14
FOR J = I + 1 TO NP: C(I, J) = C(I, J) / X: NEXT         15
FOR K = 1 TO NP: IF K = I THEN GOTO NEXK                 16
X = C(K, I): V(K) = V(K) - X * V(I)                      17
FOR J = I + 1 TO NP                                      18
C(K, J) = C(K, J) - X * C(I, J): NEXT J                  19
NEXK: NEXT K: NEXT I                                     20
PRINT " Node  Voltage"                                   21
FOR I = 1 TO NP                                          22
PRINT USING a$; I; : PRINT USING b$; V(I): NEXT I        23
PRINT " Element  Current"                                24
FOR K = 1 TO NE: I = NN(K, 1): J = NN(K, 2)             25
Q = -(V(J) - V(I)) / R                                   26
PRINT USING a$; I; J; : PRINT USING b$; Q: NEXT         27
```

```
DATA 4,4,2                                              28
DATA 1,2,1, 1,3,1, 2,4,1, 3,4,1                         29
DATA 1,1, 4,0                                           30
```

The data appended to the program (lines 28 - 30) is for the problem of Figure 25.1 for which the solution is $V_2 = V_3 = 0.5$ and currents = 0.5 for each element.

The data for the hierarchy network of Figure 14.1 is
```
DATA 7,6,5
DATA 1,2,1, 1,3,1, 2,4,1, 2,5,1, 3,6,1, 3,7,1
DATA 1,100, 4,0, 5,0, 6,0, 7,0
```

Input-Output Analysis

As further example of a network, the following section is from the Microeconomics chapter of *The Scientific MBA* (Mohr, 2017).

Input-output analysis was developed by Wassily Leontief at Harvard in 1931 and his study of the US economy with it gained a Nobel Prize and later Laurence Klein applied IOA to the world economy, also receiving a Nobel Prize (Klein et al, 1992).

At a basic level IOA analyses the interdependence of various industries. Consider, for example, three companies X, Y and Z that sell/buy products/materials to/from each other, the value of these transactions over some regular period being shown in Table ME2.

Table ME2. Input-output analysis data

	Purchases				Total
	X	**Y**	**Z**	**External**	**Output ($)**
Sales					
X	-	60	40	100	200
Y	40	-	100	260	400
Z	50	100	-	50	200
Labour	110	240	60	-	410
Total input	200	400	200	410	1,210

This table also includes labour costs for the period, as well as *external* sales (other than to the other two companies). Then company Y, for example, sells $40 of goods to X and $100 to Z, the remaining $260 of its total output ($400) being sold externally.

To produce this output Y purchases $60 in goods from X and $100 from Z, also spending $240 on labour costs.

Then from Table ME2 we can easily calculate *input coefficients* by dividing the three X,Y,Z columns by their totals, giving the results shown in Table ME3.

Table ME3. Input coefficients.

	X	Y	Z
X	-	0.15	0.2
Y	0.2	-	0.5
Z	0.25	0.25	-
Labour	0.55	0.6	0.3

Then for company Y, for example, Table ME3 shows that for each $1 of output produced 15 cents is spent on purchases from X, 25 cents on purchases from Z and 60 cents is spent on labour costs.

Then using the coefficients of Table ME3 we can write the outputs x, y, z for companies X, Y, Z as

$$(ME18a) \quad x = 0.15y + 0.20z + 100$$

$$(ME18b) \quad y = 0.20x + 0.50z + 260$$

$$(ME18c) \quad z = 0.25x + 0.25y + 50$$

Now suppose we wish to determine the effect of increasing the external sales of X to $120 (from $100). Then we change the last number in Eqn ME18a and rearrange the equations to give:

$$(ME19) \quad \begin{bmatrix} 1 & -0.15 & -0.20 \\ -0.20 & 1 & -0.50 \\ -0.25 & -0.25 & 1 \end{bmatrix} \begin{Bmatrix} x \\ y \\ x \end{Bmatrix} = \begin{Bmatrix} 120 \\ 260 \\ 50 \end{Bmatrix}$$

Solving these equations using the routine given in the following section we obtain:

$$x = \$222.84, \quad y = \$408.48, \quad z = \$207.83$$

From these results we are then, for example, able to calculate the increased labour costs resulting for each company as:

X:	223 x 0.55 = 122.7	(increase of $12.7)
Y:	408 x 0.60 = 244.8	(increase of $4.8)
Z:	208 x 0.30 = 62.4	(increase of $2.4)

Here a 'flow through' effect to other companies is immediately apparent (a more superficial approach would predict the increase in labour cost for X as increase in external output (20) multiplied by 0.55 = $11 and effects on other companies would be neglected).

Solution of matrix equations

The following simple QBASIC program solves the foregoing Input-output analysis problem using Gauss reduction, the coding for which is given in section NM4 of *The Scientific MBA* (Mohr, 2017).

```
2 REM GJR routine
4 N = 3
6 DIM SSM(N, N), Q(N), SOL(N)
8 FOR I = 1 TO N: FOR J = 1 TO N: READ SSM(I, J): NEXT: NEXT
9 FOR I = 1 TO N: READ Q(I): NEXT
10 FOR I = 1 TO N
20 X = SSM(I, I): Q(I) = Q(I) / X
30 FOR J = I+1 TO N
40 SSM(I, J) = SSM(I, J) / X: NEXT
50 FOR K = 1 TO N
60 IF K = I THEN 100
70 X = SSM(K, I): Q(K) = Q(K) - X * Q(I)
80 FOR J = I+1 TO N
90 SSM(K, J) = SSM(K, J) - X * SSM(I, J): NEXT J
100 NEXT K: NEXT I
140 FOR I = 1 TO N: PRINT Q(I): NEXT
150 END
```

```
200 DATA 1, -0.15, -0.20
210 DATA -0.2,1,-0.5
220 DATA -0.25,-0.25,1
230 DATA 120, 260, 50
```

Networking styles

Adam Grant discusses 3 networking styles: *giver, taker,* and *matcher,* suggesting that 'givers' put others ahead of themselves, whereas 'takers' always put their own interests first, whilst most people are 'matchers' who seek "a fair return for whatever they put out (Grant, 2013).

It is the takers that we tend to notice most, people like Donald Trump being a notable example, but according to Grant but it is the givers that, sometimes at least, tend to achieve most, though as often as not they will also unsuccessful.

The present authors, therefore, conclude that one should generally be a matcher, but try to be seen as a giver, and have some *balance* in how one deals with people.

Conclusion

The simple four-element network of Figure 23.1 is provides a simple example of a DC network, the following BASIC program then being able to be used to determine the nodal voltages of the 'hierarchical network' of Figure 14.1.

The Input-Output Analysis example of Table ME2 and the BASIC program given for it, illustrate modeling of financial and product exchanges between a network of companies.

Such modeling can also be used to model information exchanges within a network of organizations.

'Networking' of information is, of course, very important in both politics and business, and in personal life careful sharing of information can help advance one's career, as in politics sometimes to the detriment of other competitors.

Whilst the BASIC programs given here may not be directly useful to most readers, they are included to give a stronger 'feel' for networking and its importance that is perhaps more relevant what has sometimes been called 'age of the computer'.

PART VI
CONCLUSIONS

Chapter 24

IMPROVING LIFE

A tremendous number of people in America work very hard at something that bores them. Even a rich man thinks he has to go down to the office every day. Not because he likes it but because he can't think of anything else to do.
W. H. Auden, The Table Talk of W. H. Auden, "November 16, 1946" (comp. by Alan Ansen, ed. by Nicholas Jenkins, 1990).

Introduction

When one undertakes a self-assessment such as those of Tables 2.1 and 6.2 and finds one or two aspect of one's life need improvement, it is best to begin thinking about how to improve those aspects as soon as possible, taking any advice and offers from friends etc. along the way.

Being 'less than happy' and underpaid etc. in your current job, for example, is a major issue that will probably affect most other aspects of your life, including health and wealth, happiness, quality of family life etcetera. If that is the case producing a half-way good CV and beginning the search for another job, or perhaps giving though to starting one's own business, perhaps with some financial help from extended family.

Alternatively, one might have been living in the same place for several years and want to move, perhaps to live closer to work to make life easier for yourself, and perhaps the rest of the family.

Whatever the life improvement you seek, it is best to for it as well as possible, and following sections make a few suggestions that might be helpful to some readers.

Dealing with problems at work

If you are having problems at work, whether these be boredom with the job, finding it too hard, or finding being too low in the hierarchy to hard, then using a simple table like that of Table 24.1 might be a good start in dealing with the issue.

Table 24.1. Action plan re. job.

Item		Actions	Timing
1	Job	Stay Look for another job	1-2 years Now
2	Pay	Ask for a pay rise	Now
3	Boss	Talk to boss Make complaint	Next week In 3 months
4	Conditions	Talk to union Talk to boss	Next month In 3 months
5	Workmates	Meeting to raise issues	Next month

Table 24.1 illustrates an action plan to improve the work situation with one or two actions suggested for each of the five work items, including an approximate timing for each action.

Perhaps the key item is 1, where the plan is the cautious and sensible one of staying for a couple of years, but beginning to look for another job immediately – sensible because, of course, it can take a long time to find a job, and even longer to find a better one.

Most important, however, is that a simple plan such as this is far wiser than, for example, impatiently barging into the boss's office and abusing him about being underpaid, not an entirely unheard of situation.

Furthermore, having a sensible plan gives one hope for the immediate and medium term, as well as time to come up with other ideas to improve one's work situation, and to obtain help and advice from others on it.

Job searching

When searching for a job it is, of course, important to jhave a good Curriculum Vitae (CV).

This might have the following sections:

- ➢ A short summary section of about 10 lines.
- ➢ A table summarizing you professional experience with column 1 = type of experience , column 2 = details of this, entries in this being, for example, management, sales etcetera.
- ➢ A table summarizing your work experience with column 1 = years (e.g. 2012-2018), column 2 = company you worked for, and a line or two on what work you did. This might include, for example, any voluntary work, work you did privately to help friends or relatives, or writing work you did at home.
- ➢ For an academic, for example, a list of courses given, and perhaps another on publications in journals etc.
- ➢ A list of any organizations you belong to: for example the local branch of a political party, a charitable organization etc.
- ➢ A list of any special achievements.
- ➢ A list of any awards you have received.
- ➢ A list or table of any good comments you have received throughout life.
- ➢ The contact details of 3 referees, including at least one of your last bosses, if you are young one of your school teachers or University, TAFE etc. lecturers, and perhaps a 'personal referee' to attest to your good character etc.

At least once in life, it might be well worth paying a professional CV writer such as those who advertise in the local newspapers, and some of these will often also give advice on how to get a job, interview well etcetera.

Referees and job references

In choosing who to nominate as referees one should be careful to consider several factors, including:

> ➤ Preferably one should be 'relevant' in some way to the job in question.
> ➤ They should be people you trust.
> ➤ Always ask for an 'upfront' referee statement to be given to you, and take it to the interview and quote the best lines from it.
> ➤ Often the organization offering the job will get a 'confidential' referee statement from a past boss, either over the phone or by email. Always ask at interview for a copy of (or what was said if verbal) these references. If they differ significantly from the upfront statement you got then this proves that ex boss is dishonest/a liar.
> ➤ When you have references from two past bosses, point out that the best reference should be that considered.
> ➤ Get past colleagues to give you a 'statement' about any past boss you use as referee. If this is weak or somewhat negative, that will help overcome any negativity that he might have said about you in confidence.

For personal referees, who are usually friends etc., the latter step should not be necessary.

The first author was a sad case in point, using a bastard ex-boss who had bullied him into resigning as referee for several years, until he woke up to the fact that he had still been calling him a "lousy lecturer", but now not in the corridor, but in confidential referee statements. The second had been his PhD supervisor in Cambridge, and also in the same department at Auckland U for most of his time there, but was probably telling people confidentially that the author did not have a job, and after 2+ years this was killing off his prospects [for the first couple of years he was stuck dealing with 2 ailing parents which was too depressing to talk about – but he should have told this story as it should have been seen as a positive.

Finally, to compound the problem, he did not use the other bad boss of his life, whose name he put on a book he managed to get out a couple of years after quitting in Auckland. This person should have, been used, or at least somebody else from the department of which he was HOD (this he did eventually did do, but far too many years late).

Candidate selection

When you are searching for a job it is best to be aware of how selection committees choose who to interview, and how they then chose who to give the job to after the interviews have been completed.

Choosing who to give the job to is often done on a somewhat quantitative basis using a process of summing *weighted attributes*.

Table 24.2.

Job candidate selection using weighted attribute scores.

Attribute	Weight	Score			Weighted score		
		Tom	Dick	Harry	Tom	Dick	Harry
Qualific-ations	2	8	5	3	16	10	6
Experience	3	5	7	6	15	21	18
Age	1	5	5	8	5	5	8
Interview	2	3	5	8	6	10	16
Referees	1	5	5	5	5	5	5
Total					46	51	53

A good example is the task of selecting the 'best' of three candidates Tom, Dick and Harry, for a job using the *decision table* of Table 24.2.

Here five attributes: qualifications, experience (relevant), age (or total experience), impression made at interview and strength of recommendations made by referees, are used and each of these is given a weight in the second column.

Then the three candidates are given a score out of ten for each attribute by each member of the selection panel and the results averaged (to the nearest round number for simplicity here), giving the results shown in columns 3,4,5.

Finally, these scores are multiplied by the weights, giving the results of columns 6, 7, & 8 and these figures are summed to give the totals shown.

The final result indicates Harry as the best candidate.

In practice, however, it is best to include other considerations such as:

[1] Who top scored in the most important attributes?

[2] If the candidate is an existing employee (in another position) has there been any bias?

In this sort of analysis the choice of attributes is crucial, as is their weighting, so that such factors can also be reviewed before making a final decision.

Job seekers would do well, of course, to be aware of the decision-making process illustrated in Table 24.2, for example making a special effort to emphasize their previous work experience, especially *relevant* work experience, and also such factors as the *breadth*, *'quality'* and *duration* of their work history, putting more emphasis on 'quality rather than quantity' of their qualifications and experience if they are younger applicants.

Starting you own business – case study 1

The following case study is from the first chapter/subject of *The Scientific* MBA (Mohr, 2017).

Case study: beginning as a one man business

In his mid 20s Jim joined a US manufacturer of specialist medical equipment as, he thought, a sales manager selling a single item with no competition.

The job description led him to believe that he would be in charge of a few sales staff but he found himself the sole representative in the UK.

He stuck it out for five years, however, by which time he was competing with equipment from 20 other companies and needed to be selling a product range rather than a single piece of specialist equipment to make a living.

Following a suggestion from a friend, Jim decided to become an independent agent for the single item of the US company, adding a small range of other manufacturer's products to his stock, and taking out a smallish loan for this purpose.

Things soon went much better and his bank offered him a larger loan that would allow him to add more lines and employ a salesperson. Should he accept?

Deciding to expand

Jim was advised to base his decision on:

a. His main business objectives.
b. Predicted sales of new lines based on his experience.
c. A cash flow forecast for his predicted sales volume.

He listed his main objectives as:

1. Maximum *sales* (not profit), at least in the short term.
2. *Growth* into a larger company with comfortable offices.
3. Enough *profit* to provide a satisfactory living.
4. The *welfare* of the sick on whom his medical equipment was used.

He also decided that appropriate marketing policies for these objectives would be low margins and product diversity, to which end he had several new lines in mind.

Based on these considerations the decision was obviously to accept the loan offer, stock a wider range and employ and extra man. His business has continued to grow ever since.

He now has a typical *small business* with a manager (himself), a secretary, a sales manager and several sales representatives.

Starting you own business – case study 2

The following case study is given in the chapter entitled "The Second Door" in the book *Life In Half a Second* (Michalewicz, 2013).

The case is that of a young man Jud who, at the age of 18, developed a "prototype for contextual search on a mobile phone". Hoping to commercialize this invention, after graduating from high school, he flew to Silicon Valley in the late 1990s searching for an investor. After being rejected 57 times he was about to give up when he finally found an investor willing to back his invention financially.

Jud developed his prototype further, and success followed, Michalewicz calling him "one of my favourite entrepreneurs".

Starting you own business – case study 3

Bill Gates started Microsoft with friend Paul Allen when he was just 19, after dropping out of Harvard. By then, having spent the previous few years working on a "primitive" computer at school, he was already a competent programmer. Indeed, in his final year at school he was offered a job (with Allen) to debug a defence contractor's computer system (Butler-Bowdon, 2017).

Gates and Allen had thought about starting their own software company for years, but his parents wanted him to complete a University course. According to Butler-Bowdon (2017): "- - when he duly arrived in Harvard his intention was to find people who were smarter than he was. Disappointed, he spent a lot of time playing poker in addition to some maths courses."

According to Wallace and Erickson (1992):

At Harvard, Gates read business books like other male students read Playboy. He wanted to know everything he could about running a company, from managing people to marketing products.

When Gates and Allen read about a new personal computer called the 'Altair' being made by a company in New Mexico they convinced it to let them write a version of BASIC for it. Subsequently they wrote versions of BASIC for big companies such as General Electric and National Cash Register, then clinching a deal with IBM in 1981 – and the rest is history from that point, the first author writing in *The Scientific MBA* (Mohr, 2017):

BASIC was developed by Kemeny and Kurtz at Dartmouth College (New Hampshire) in the early 1960s and was much used on minicomputers (which typically had 16 terminals, each being allowed 16 kb of RAM, the amount required by the then versions of BASIC) in the 1970s. In 1975 the first microcomputer was sold, a clumsy box + switches affair with storage of only 256 bytes. In the same year Tiny BASIC, consisting of just 20 pages of code, was written and many versions of this quickly appeared and, also in 1975, Gates and Allen launched Microsoft Corporation with their version, this being marketed with the Altair microcomputer. In the early 1980s IBM quit their almost monopoly of the electric ('golfball') typewriter market, switching to production of PCs, the first IBM PC having 16 kb of RAM.

Gates was lucky, however, for in 1983 the American Planning Corporation and Christopher Cochran produced a better version of BASIC than Microsoft had at that time called MegaBasic.

Megabasic came with two versions, one with 8 digit computation, and the other 14, whereas FORTRAN and BASIC still used 7 digits (effectively 6.7) for "single precision" computation, and 16 digits for "double precision." The 8 digit choice for Megabasic was the more sensible option as one was far less likely to ever need slower double precision computation, and when one did 14 digits was a better option.

The program names for the 2 MegaBasics were MSDBAS08.exe and MSDBAS14.exe, leading the first author to suspect 'MSD' might have stood for Microsoft Development Basic.

MegaBasic, however, had limited success, whereas Microsoft went from strength to strength with a BASIC for the first IBM PC's, then GWBASIC, then QBASIC, then QuickBasic (QBASIC with a compiler), then several versions of Visual Basic, along with versions 1 – 6 of the MSDOS operating system, followed by several versions of the Windows operating system.

Microsoft won out in the end, of course, because of its link with IBM, who made with first co-called "personal computer" circa 1982, one which the best part of 1MB of RAM, much more than earlier "microcomputers" had, for example around the same time the "Spectravideo" had a total of 128 kb of memory, but only 32 kb of this was really 'free', the rest being used to store the operating system.

The bottom line: You need to bit of luck to 'hit the big time'.

Improving family life

Improvements in family life might include:

➢ Moving house so that you or your wife live closer to work.

➢ Moving house so your children are closer to school.

➢ Changing school for your children, perhaps so they are close to home which has many advantages.

➢ Improving family health with improved diet, exercise, and lifestyle routines.

➢ Improving family recreation options to healthier and perhaps cheaper ones close to home.

➢ Improving the family's social life.

Conclusion

There are many things one can do to improve life, and thereby perhaps make life more successful, and only a few examples have been considered in the preceding chapter.

Many others were given in preceding chapters, however, and a couple more are given in the following chapter.

Chapter 25

CONCLUSIONS

There are many paths to the top of the mountain,
but the view is always the same.
Chinese Proverb

If A is a success in life, then A equals x plus y plus z. Work
is x; y is play; and z is keeping your mouth shut.
Albert Einstein, quoted in: Observer, London, 15 Jan. 1950.

Positivity to improve life

Taking a more positive, optimistic outlook is one of the keys to success, whereas negative-minded people tend to say: "It won't work" etcetera to most propositions and ideas.

The following table gives some examples of how to turn negative thinking into positive thinking, including examples suggested by Kemp (2014).

Table 25.1. Turning negativity into positivity

Negative self-talk	Positive self-talk
I've never done it before.	It's a chance to learn something.
It's too hard.	I'll try and make it easier.
I don't have the time.	I'll try and fit it into my plans.
I'm too tired.	I'll try and make the effort.
It won't work.	Let's try anyway.
It's too radical a change.	So much the better
Nobody talks to me.	I'll keep trying.

The bottom line here is that it is often best 'to give it a try' when it comes to things that might improves one's life at home or in the workplace.

Optimism improves health

A team of psychologists, having done preliminary experiments with rats that showed the 'helplessness' weakened the body, studied 120 men who had had a first heart attack (Kemp, 2014).

The interviewed the men extensively to rate their optimism, counting the "because" statements they used to explain events in their lives. They found that none of the usual risk factors such as blood pressure, cholesterol levels, or how extensive the damage from the first heart attack was, predicted death, but that "only the men's level of optimism eight and a half years earlier predicted a second heart attack."

Of the 16 most pessimistic men, 15 died, whereas of the 16 most optimistic men, only 5 died.

The results of this a study of 999 people aged from 65 to 85 which began in 1991 in the Netherland.

The meta-study "Optimism and Physical Health" analyzed 83 separate studies of the relationship between optimism and physical health, 18 of which involved 2,858 patients and their cancer history. The results gave "robust" support to the notion that more optimistic people had better cancer outcomes (Kemp, 2014).

A recent German study that 'priming' of people to increase their confidence resulted in a 35% better chance of their succeeding (ABC2 TV news report, ^PM, 16/6/2018).

The bottom line here, of course, is that not only will optimism improve quality of life, and the likelihood of success in life, but it also improves both mental and physical health.

Perseverance needed for success

Angela Duckworth, believing that talent was overrated as the main factor for success, proposed that one should be both talented and hardworking for best results, summarizing this as (Duckworth, 2016):

1. Talent x *effort* = skill
2. Skill x *effort* = achievement

Becoming a leader

In his book *On Becoming a Leader* Warren Bennis says that becoming a leader involves (Bennis, 1989):

> Curiosity and continuous learning.
> A compelling vision.
> The ability to communicate that vision.
> Being prepared to take a risk.
> Personal integrity: maturity, open to criticism etc.
> Allowing time to think and plan.
> Seeking success in small increments, not one 'big rush'.

One also requires, of course, some of the other key attributes discussed in the present book, including optimism, perseverance, patience and wisdom (Gracian, 1647).

Self-assessment

Accurate self-assessment is, of course, very important in helping pinpoint problems, and in solving them, and Table 2.1, 6.1 and 16.1 give example of such self-assessment, whilst the expectancy-value and information integration methods of attitude evaluation may also be useful in this context.

The 2017 book *Success: The Psychology of Achievement* gives a "daily diary" which includes such items as those shown in Table 25.2 [we suggest that this need only be done monthly] shown on the following page.

In assessing just about anything, and any aspect of life, Mohr's Metrology, which is the 10th law of Mohronism, and which is briefly outlined in the following section, is also useful (Mohr & Fear, 2015; Mohr et al., 2018d).

Table 25.2. Daily record of progress etc.

Item	Results	Action needed
Progress	What achieved?	New goals?
Affect on others	Positive?	Any regrets?
Reputation	Increase?	Anything needing fix?
Support	Who supported me?	Who else might?
Supporting others	People I helped.	Who should I help?
Time	Did I waste time?	Avoid next time
Problems solved	What fixed?	What needs fixing?
Skills, connections etc.	Increased?	What needs increase?
Personal life	OK?	New goals?

Mohr's Metrology

This requires a little elaboration. It asserts that all human traits can be measured. Madness, for example, is not a black and white thing, and we should be given a score, though this may vary a little according to such factors as the weather and countless others that hardly need mention.

For this law we use the **Mohr Scale**, noting that a score of 10 is not possible as perfect madness, for example, would surely be rapidly terminal. Furthermore a score of zero is not possible as perfect sanity would surely constitute insanity.

In the case of general health, or how much alive one is, 0 would be dead (not a valid health score), whilst 10 would be too good to be true (also not a valid health score).

Hence the Mohr Scale is 1 - 9, and the median score is the sum of the possible scores divided by the number of possible scores, that is $45/9 = 5$. This is the median score with four possible scores above and below it. With this score you don't pass or fail but are borderline.

The Mohr scale is also useful in the study of *ethics* where the questions of what is 'right' or 'good' are put, quickly followed by the question: "how good?" For this purpose the Mohr scale provides a set of ordinal numbers where, for example, 9 is the maximum goodness (10 would be too good to be true).

As an example, the first author (now 73) recently asked an ex-colleague circa 5 years older what his score was, and he said 8, which was perhaps slightly optimistic.

Money and wealth

Mohr's Law of Capitalism was discussed in Chapter 14, being of a hierarchical nature and thus leading to an exponential result, explaining how in capitalism the rich get richer, and the poor get poorer, which has been the case throughout most of the world for most of history, and certainly in the last decade or more also.

The pigs in Orwell's *Animal Farm* are the fat capitalists, of course, but in the 2017 book *Success: The Psychology of Achievement,* it is claimed that whilst US gross GNP tripled from between 1947 to 1998, life satisfaction remained approximately constant, in line with clichés such as *money isn't everything.*

The bottom line here, of course, is that success involves achieving a wide variety of things, ranging from winning sporting contests (perhaps as an amateur), to getting a good job or making (enough at least) money.

Slow down, don't overstress

Cheryl Richardson suggest that often we should "slow down to succeed", allowing ourselves regular 'downtime' because we "all need a holiday from thinking too much", and try to lessen the impact of things in life that we find stressful and worrying (Richardson, 1998).

The Yerkes-Dodson law of arousal suggests that there is an optimum stress level at which we perform best, and to be *in the zone* for a purely intellectual activity such as reading a book we need only a low stress level, to be in the zone for activities that combine physical and intellectual performance a medium stress level is needed, whilst purely physical activities may involve higher stress levels, if they are very competitive *fight or flight* hormones sometimes having negative effects such as shrinking the hippocampus, reducing self-control, memory function, and emotional regulation.

Conclusions

For best results one must, of course, tackle life and its occasional problems with the inter-related personal characteristics and behaviours:

> - Self-esteem.
> - Self-confidence.
> - Self-reliance.
> - Self-belief.
> - Self-regulation or control.
> - Self-assessment in similar fashion to the Expectation-Value and Information Integration models of attitude formation and assessment.
> - Realistic goal-setting.
> - Support from friends etc. with problems, and in achieving one's goals.

Then, if one has self-confidence, achievable goals etc., one might have a good chance of success.

One bottom line, trivial as it may seem, is that, as Macy emphasizes (Macy, 2015):

Never quit . . . except when you should quit.

Another more important one is creativity, as emphasized in our definition of Real IQ in Chapter 10, and according to Wallace Wattles (Wattles, 1910):

Consider that other people can't 'beat you to it' if you are creating something unique out of imagination, skills, and experience that make up your own personality.

and that to succeed you must provide people with results that are seen as greater in value than the financial etc. resources used.

Another important point is the question if honesty. For example, I once had an English lady friend who always put her age down 10 years on her CV, telling me once:

You have to lie to get jobs.

OK up to a point, perhaps, and in politics, of course, 'pollies' spout BS most of the time.

One example of circa 5/10 honesty on the Mohr Scale (of 1 to 9) was Robert Menzies calling his new Australian political party the Liberal Party, borrowing the name of the third largest party in England at the time (circa 1950 as best we can recall right now). In fact, the Liberal Party of Australia is a *conservative party,* so there was some degree of dishonesty in the name choice, a choice which, however, proved to be a very successful one!

One way to try and summarize a few of the *keys* to happiness and success in life is to make a mnemonic using the word *optimism,* for example:

O = optimism

P = perseverance

T = time (allow enough), or (give it a) try

I = intelligence

M = mediation

I = intuition

S = skill

M = meticulousness

The reader, of course, should feel free to develop mnemonics of his or her own that might help in their pursuit of success, for example, using a company name for which an appropriate mnemonic conveys a useful message.

To conclude this book, however, we shall quote 'the bard', William Shakespeare:

JAQUES. All the world's a stage.
And all the men and women merely players;
They have their exits and entrances;
And one man in his time plays many parts;
His acts being of seven ages.
As You Like It (1599), Act 2, Scene 7.

25. Conclusions

Those 7 ages could be deemed to be:

1. Infancy.
2. Childhood.
3. Schooldays.
4. Training, apprenticeship etc.
5. Working life – first stage.
6. Working life – second stage +.
7. Old age, retirement etc.

Then, for example, stage 5 above would be one's first full-time job, perhaps in the vocation for which one trained, whilst stage 6 might then be moving on to a better job, starting one's own business etcetera, and perhaps achieving greater SUCCESS in life by doing do.

The End

References

Allport GW, *The Nature of Prejudice,* Addison-Wesley, Reading MA (1954).

Anthony, R (Dr), *The Ultimate Secrets of Total Self-Confidence, Master the Simple Step-by-step principles and change your life,* John Blake, London (2010).

Atrens D, Curthoys I, *The Neurosciences and Behaviour: An Introduction,* 2nd edn, Academic Press, Sydney (1982).

Baddeley A, *Human Memory, Theory and Practice,* Lawrence Erlbaum Associates, Hove, UK (1990).

Bennis, Warren, *On Becoming a Leader* (1989).

Blanchard, Kenneth; Johnson, Spencer, *The One Minute Manager* (1981).

Borushek A, *Allan Borushek's Calorie, Fat & Carbohydrate Counter,* Hinkler Books, Melbourne, 2014.

Borushek A, Borushek J, *The Complete Australian Heart Disease Prevention Manual.* Family Health Publications, Perth, 1981.

Brickman P, Redfield J, Harrison AA, Crandell R, Drive and predisposition as factors in the attitudinal effects of mere exposure, *Journal of Experimental Social Psychology* 8 (1972) 31-44.

Burrell A, Broker bastardization no laughing matter for juniors and "Jew Boys", *Australian Financial Review,* 7 Feb. 2001, p. MW16.

Butler-Bowden, Tom, *50 Psychology Classics,* 2nd edition, Nicholas Brealey Publishing, London (2017).

Butler-Bowden, Tom, *50 Success Classics,* 2nd edition, Nicholas Brealey Publishing, London (2017b).

Carter P, *IQ and Psychometric Tests* 2nd edn, Kogan Page, London (2007).

Christensen A, *Heart Health: An American Yoga Association Wellness Guide.* Twin Streams Books, New York, 2001.

Cooke JP (with J Zimmer), *The Cardiovascular Cure.* Broadway Books, New York, 2002.

Corder R, *The Red Wine Diet.* Sphere, London, 2007.

Craughwell, Thomas J, *How Smart Are You?, Test Your IQ,* Black Dog & Leventhal, New York NY (2012).

De Bono E, *Lateral Thinking for Management,* Pelican, Harmondsworth (1982).

Angela Duckworth, *Grit: The Power of Passion and Perseverance* (2016).

Eagly AH, Chaiken S, *The Psychology of Attitudes,* Harcourt Brace Jovanovich, Orlando FA (1993).

Forbes HD, *Ethnic Conflict: Commerce, Culture, and the Contact Hypothesis,* Yale University Press, New Haven (1997).

Foss DJ, Hakes DT, *Psycholinguistics: An Introduction to the Psychology of Language,* Prentice-Hall, Englewood Cliffs NJ (1978).

Gladwell, Malcolm, *Outliers: The Story of Success* (2008).

Goodall (van Lawick-Goodall) J, *In the Shadow of Man,* Houghton-Mifflin, Boston (1971).

Gracian, Baltasar, *The Art of Worldly Wisdom* (1647).

Grant Adam, *Give and Take* (2013).

Healey J (ed.), *Issues in Society Vol. 330, 'Dealing With Bullying',* the Spinney Press, Thirroul NSW (2011).

Heyn EV, *Fires of Genius, Inventors of the Past Century,* Anchor Press/Doubleday, Garden City, New York (1976).

Holford C, Colson D, *Optimum Nutrition For Your Child,* Piatkus, London (2008).

Jochems R, *Dr Moerman's Anti-Cancer Diet.* Avery, New York, 1990.

Kaplan M, Kaplan E, *Bozo Sapiens, Why to Err is Human,* Bloomsbury, New York (2010).

Kemp, Jurrian, *The Intelligent Optimist's Guide to Life: How to Find Health and Success in a World That's a Better Place Than You Think,* Berret-Koehler Publishers Inc., San Francisco (2014).

Kiefer C, Constable M, *The Art of Insight, How to have more AHA! moments,* Bennet-Koehler, San Francisco (2013).

Kirchler E, Zani B, Why don't they stay at home? Prejudices against ethnic minorities in Italy, *Journal of Community and Applied Social Psychology* 5 (1995) 59-65.

Klein LR, Pauly P, Voison P, The world economy - a global model. *Perspectives in Computing* 2 (1982).

Kowalski RE, *The 8-Week Cholesterol Cure,* Schwartz, Sydney, 1987.

Krapp K, editor, *Psychologists & Their Theories for Students,* vol. 1: A-K, Thomson Gale, Farmington Hills, MI (2005).

Kurzweil R, *The 10% Solution for a Healthy Life, How to Eliminate Virtually All Risk of Heart Disease and Cancer.* Bookman Press, Melbourne, 1993.

Likert R, *New Patterns of Management,* McGraw-Hill, New York (1961).

Lindzey G, Hall CS, Thompson RF, *Psychology,* 2nd edn, Worth, New York (1978).

Lopez. Shane J., *Making Hope Happen, Create The Future You Want for Yourself and Others,* Atria, New York (2013).

Macinnis P, *100 Discoveries, The greatest breakthroughs in history,* Pier 9, Sydney (2009).

Mackintosh NJ, *IQ and Human Intelligence*, 2nd ed., Oxford University Press, Oxford (2011).

Macy, Travis, *The Ultra Mindset: An Endurance Champion's 8 Core Principles for Success in Business, Sports, and Life*, De Capo Press, Philadelphia PA (2015).

Marchese R, Hill A, *The Essential Guide to Fitness for the fitness instructor*, Pearson/Prentice-Hall, Sydney, 2005.

Marks B, Marks R, Spillane R, *The Management Contradictory*, Michelle Anderson Publishing, Melbourne (2006).

McGowan MP, *Heart Fitness for Life.* Oxford University Press, New York, 1998.

McGraw, Phil, *Family First: Your Step-by-Step Plan for Creating a Phenomenal Family,* Free Press/Simon & Schuster Inc., New York NY (2004).

Michalewicz, Matthew, *Life In Half a Second: How to achieve success before it's too late.* Hybrid Publishers, Melbourne, 2013.

Mohr GA, *Design of Plate and Shell Structures using Finite Elements,* PhD thesis , University of Cambridge (1976).

Mohr GA, *The Finite Element Method for Solids, Fluids, and Optimization,* OUP Oxford (1992).

Mohr GA, *The Doomsday Calculation, The End of the Human Race,* Xlibris, Sydney (2012a).

Mohr GA, *The War of the Sexes, Women Are Getting On Top,* Xlibris, Sydney (2012b).

Mohr GA, *Curing Cancer & Heart Disease, Proven Ways to Combat Aging, Atherosclerosis & Cancer,* Xlibris, Sydney (2012c).

Mohr GA, *Heart Disease, Cancer & Aging, Proven Neutraceutical and Lifestyle Solutions,* Horizon Publishing Group, Sydney (2013a).

Mohr GA, *The Pretentious Persuaders, A Brief History & Science of Mass Persuasion,* 2nd edn, Horizon Publishing Group, Sydney (2013b).

Mohr GA, *The History & Psychology of Human Conflicts,* Horizon Publishing Group, Sydney (2014a).

Mohr GA, *Elementary Thinking for the 21st Century,* Xlibris, Sydney (2014b).

Mohr GA, Sinclair R, Fear E, *The Evolving Universe, Relativity, Redshift and Life From Space,* Xlibris, Sydney (2014).

Mohr GA, Fear E, *World Religions, The History, Psychology, Issues & Truth,* Xlibris, Sydney (2015).

Mohr GA, *The 8-Week+ Program to Reverse Cardiovascular Disease,* Book Venture, Ishpeming MI (2015).

Mohr GA, *The Scientific MBA,* 5th edn, *Balboa Press,* Bloomington IN (2017).

Mohr GA, Sinclair R, Fear R, *Human Intelligence, Learning & behavior,* Inspiring Publishers, Canberra (2017).

Mohr GA, *The DIY Cardiovascular Cure: A Comprehensive Program to Reverse Atherosclerosis,* Amazon-Kindle (2018a).

Mohr GA, *Combating Cancer: Proven Neutraceutical & Lifestyle Solutions,* Amazon-Kindle (2018b).

Mohr GA, *The War of the Sexes, The Problems & the Solutions,* Amazon-Kindle (2018c).

Mohr GA, *Elementary Thinking for Modern Management,* Amazon-Kindle (2018d).

Mohr GA, *Mohr's Law of Hierarchies, and many other Mohr's Laws,* Amazon-Kindle (2018e).

Mohr GA, Mohr RS, Mohr PE, *The Psychology of Hope,* Balboa Press, Bloomington IN (2018).

Mohr GA, Mohr RS, Mohr PE, *New Theories of the Universe, Evolution and Relativity,* Amazon-Kindle (2018a).

References

Mohr GA, Mohr PE, Mohr RS, *The Population Explosion*, Amazon-Kindle (2018b).

Mohr GA, Mohr RS, Mohr PE, *Human Conflict: An Attitudinal Psychology Model*, Amazon-Kindle (2018c).

Mohr GA, Mohr PE, Mohr RS, *World Religions: From Animism to Mohronism*, Amazon-Kindle (2018d).

Mohr GA, Mohr PE, Mohr RS, *Brainwashed Zombies: Religious, Political & Consumer Persuasion*, Amazon-Kindle (2018e).

Morgan CT, King RA, Robinson NM, *Introduction to Psychology*, 6th edn, McGraw-Hill, Tokyo (1979).

Murray F, *Program Your Heart for Health.* Larchmont Books, New York, 1977.

Newcomb TM, Persistence and regression of changed attitudes, *Journal of Sociological Issues* 19 (1963) 3-14.

Ornish D, *Dr Dean Ornish's Program for Reversing Heart Disease.* Ivy Books/Ballantine, New York, 1996.

Ostrander S, Schroeder L, *Superlearning*, Delacorte/Confucian Press, New York (1979).

Packard V, *The People Shapers,* Nelson, Melbourne (1978).

Perlman D, Oskamp S, The effects of picture content and exposure frequency on evaluations of Negroes and whites, *Journal of Experimental Social Psychology* 7 (1971) 503-514.

Peter LJ, Hull R, *The Peter Principle,* Souvenir Press, London (1969).

Phillips L, Behaving badly, *HR Monthly*, Sept. 2000, pp/ 36-37.

Renton NE, *Guide to Meetings and Organizations,* 2nd edn, The Law Book Co. Ltd, Melbourne (1972).

Richardson, Cheryl, *Take Time for Your Life: A Seven-Step Program for Creating the Life You Want* (1998).

Sargent M, *Drinking and Alcoholism in Australia: A Power Relations Theory,* Longman Cheshire, Melbourne (1979).

Schaefer TR, Contacts between immigrants and Englishmen: Road to tolerance or intolerance, *New Community* 2 (1973) 358-371.

Slaybaugh J, Pareto's Law and modern management, *Management Services,* March-April 1967.

Snyder, CR, *The Psychology of Hope, You Can Get Here From There,* Simon & Schuster, New York, NY (1994).

Sternberg RJ, *In Search of the Human Mind,* 2nd edn, Harcourt Brace College Publishers, Orlando FL (1998).

Sudy M (editor), *Personal Trainer Manual.* American Council on Exercise & Reebok University Press, San Diego, 1991.

Trump, Donald, *The Way to the Top, The Best Business Advice I Ever Received,* Crown Business, New York, NY (2004).

Vernon, PE, *Intelligence and Attainment Tests,* University of London Press, London (1960).

Wallace, James, and Erickson, Jim, *Hard Drive: Bill Gates and the Making of the Microsoft Empire* (1992).

References

THE PSYCHOLOGY OF SUCCESS

The book discusses many issues related to success in life:

➢ Deciding upon key goals, and planning to achieve them.
➢ Having self-confidence, optimism, and a positive attitude.
➢ Having a sensible, healthy, lifestyle.
➢ Continued gaining of new knowledge and skills throughout life.
➢ Continuing education and learning, and *Real IQ*.
➢ How corporations and leaders operate.
➢ The problems created by hierarchical organizational structures.
➢ How to deal with 'bad bosses'.
➢ How to ensure a good and successful home life.
➢ How to raise smarter and more successful children.
➢ Social activities, meetings, and networking.
➢ Other ways in which to improve your life and make it successful.

G. A. Mohr did his PhD at Churchill College, Cambridge. He published circa 60 papers for 20 international journals and more than 25 books, including:

A Microcomputer Introduction to the Finite Element Method
Finite Elements for Solids, Fluids, and Optimization
The Pretentious Persuaders, A Brief History & Science of Mass Persuasion
Curing Cancer & Heart Disease
The Variant Virus, Introducing Secret Agent Simon Sinclair
The Doomsday Calculation, The End Of The Human Race
Heart Disease, Cancer, & Ageing: Proven Neutraceutical & Lifestyle Solutions
2045: A Remote Town Survives Global Holocaust
The History & Psychology of Human Conflict;   The War of the Sexes
Elementary Thinking for the 21st Century
The 8-Week+ Program to Reverse Cardiovascular Disease
The Scientific MBA;   Mohr's Law of Hierarchies
The DIY Cardiovascular Cure;   Combating Cancer
Elementary Thinking for Modern Management

Also with R.S. Mohr/Richard Sinclair & P.E. Mohr/Edwin Fear:

The Evolving Universe: Relativity, Redshift and Life from Space
World Religions: The History, Psychology, Issues & Truth
World War 3, When & How Will It End?
The Brainwashed, From Consumer Zombies to Islamic Jihad
Human Intelligence, Learning & Behaviour
New Theories of The Universe, Evolution, and Relativity
The Psychology of Hope;   The Population Explosion
Brainwashed Zombies: Religious, Political & Consumer Persuasion
Human Conflict: An Attitudinal Psychology Model
World Religions: From Animism to Mohronism